OPENING LEADS

OPENING LEADS

Robert Ewen

♠ ♡ ◇ ♣

PRENTICE-HALL, INC., Englewood Cliffs, N.J.

Second printing.........October, 1970

Opening Leads by Robert Ewen

© 1970 by Robert Ewen

Copyright under International and Pan American
Copyright Conventions

Library of Congress Catalog Card Number: 73-83447

Printed in the United States of America • *T*
13-637371-2—Case
13-637363-4—Paper

Prentice-Hall International, Inc., *London*
Prentice-Hall of Australia, Pty. Ltd., *Sydney*
Prentice-Hall of Canada, Ltd., *Toronto*
Prentice-Hall of India Private Ltd., *New Delhi*
Prentice-Hall of Japan, Inc., *Tokyo*

Introduction

Bob Ewen is a young man who hasn't yet decided which of his many talents will bring him fame, fortune or both.

He is assistant professor of psychology at New York University; co-author of a monograph, *Testing and Fair Employment*, dealing with the fairness and validity of personnel tests for various ethnic groups. He achieved his Ph. D. at the University of Illinois in 1965, and in the course of his college career he won two National Intercollegiate Bridge Championships.

Since college days, Ewen has done so well in comparatively infrequent entry into bridge championship competition that he has attracted attention as one of the bright stars among younger players. He has also written several magazine articles on bridge and constructed a brand new type of bridge-word puzzle.

By some oversight of older bridge writers, Ewen is the first to concentrate a whole book on the subject of the one play that wins or loses more points than any other single factor of contract bridge—the opening lead. The result is not only a fascinating bridge book, but one sure to be worth a bushel of points to any reader.

RICHARD L. FREY

I am indebted to *The Bridge World* for permission to reproduce material that originally appeared in that magazine, and to Paul Heitner, Jeff Rubens, and Tom Smith for comments and suggestions.

Contents

1

Rate Your Opening Leads

♠ ♡ ◇ ♣

A friend of mine recently finished reading his very first bridge book. As might be expected, he was all agog about the wealth of new information that he had acquired, and most eager to put it into practice at the earliest possible moment. In less time than it takes to tell about it, three other bridge addicts were summoned by telephone and arrived at my friend's house, the cards were shuffled and dealt, and the hostilities were under way. I arrived in time to kibitz the first deal and seated myself behind my friend, ready to offer any profound comments that might assist him in his quest for bridge knowledge. His hand was:

♠ 10 9 6   ♡ J 8 6 3 2   ◇ 10 9 8   ♣ 7 4

This is hardly the sort of holding that tends to keep a kibitzer on the edge of his chair! My friend's right-hand opponent was the dealer and opened the bidding with 1 NT. My friend passed, and his left-hand opponent raised to 3 NT, ending the auction. Clearly relieved that the opponents had not bid a grand slam, my friend led the three of hearts without a second thought. "No problem here," he confided to me in a low voice. " 'Fourth from your longest and strongest suit' is what the book recommends." The play proceeded before I had a chance to reply, and the complete deal was as follows:

NORTH
♠ J 4 3
♡ Q 10 4
◇ Q J
♣ A 10 9 6 5

WEST (my friend)
♠ 10 9 6
♡ J 8 6 3 2
◇ 10 9 8
♣ 7 4

EAST
♠ K Q 7 2
♡ A 5
◇ 6 5 3 2
♣ K 8 2

SOUTH
♠ A 8 5
♡ K 9 7
◇ A K 7 4
♣ Q J 3

The bidding:

SOUTH	WEST	NORTH	EAST
1 NT	Pass	3 NT	Pass
Pass	Pass		

East won the first trick with the ace of hearts and returned a heart; South won with the king and led the queen of clubs for a finesse. It lost, but South was not dismayed, for he could not be prevented from taking the rest of the tricks.

I had a few choice comments about this result, but before I could get a word in edgewise my friend had dealt the next hand, looked at his cards, and passed with a mournful air. His luck as a card-holder certainly did seem to leave something to be desired, for his hand was:

♠ 7 4   ♡ 9 6 5 2   ◇ 5 4 3 2   ♣ K 10 4

His left-hand opponent opened the bidding with 1 ◇, and his adversaries lost no time reaching game via the following auction:

WEST	NORTH	EAST	SOUTH
Pass	1 ◇	Pass	1 ♠
Pass	3 ◇	Pass	3 ♠
Pass	4 ♠	Pass	Pass
Pass			

This opening lead caused more of a problem than the preceding one. My friend's indecision was apparent; he pulled one card halfway out of his hand, replaced it, and fingered another. I heard him mutter such things as "Never lead away from a king" and "Don't lead the opponents' suits." Suddenly, his face brightened and he came to a decision. "When in doubt, lead trumps," he whispered to me, and led the seven of spades. Unfortunately for the defenders, this pearl of knowledge that he had gleaned from his bridge book proved to be flawed, for the whole hand was:

```
                    NORTH
                    ♠ A J
                    ♡ A K
                    ◇ K Q J 9 8 6
                    ♣ 9 8 2
     WEST (my friend)              EAST
     ♠ 7 4                         ♠ K 6 2
     ♡ 9 6 5 2                     ♡ Q 10 8 4
     ◇ 5 4 3 2                     ◇ A 10
     ♣ K 10 4                      ♣ Q 7 6 3
                    SOUTH
                    ♠ Q 10 9 8 5 3
                    ♡ J 7 3
                    ◇ 7
                    ♣ A J 5
```

South gave the hand some thought, and then put up dummy's spade ace at the first trick and led the king of diamonds. East won with the ace, but the contract was impregnable. He chose to return a club; South won with the ace, led a heart to dummy's ace, cashed the queen of diamonds and discarded a losing club, and led the jack of diamonds. East found the best defense of ruffing with a low trump to stop a discard, but South simply over-ruffed, entered dummy with the heart king, and discarded his last club on the nine of diamonds. Whether or not East chose to ruff this trick, his king of spades was the last trick for the defense, and South made his contract with an overtrick.

The opponents gleefully scored up game and rubber, and my friend complained bitterly about his poor hands. This was a bit more than I could stand, however, and I decided it was time for the expert to say a word. "Your hands may be poor, but your opening leads are horrendous," I said in my usual tactful manner. "On the first hand, the correct opening lead of the ten of spades defeats the contract, for it immediately establishes three spade tricks for the defense. Declarer must risk the club finesse, because he has only eight tricks if he does not take it, and partner's club king and heart ace will give your side just enough tricks to beat the hand."

My audience was not showing quite the joy and appreciation that such an erudite lecture should have merited, but I continued on undaunted. "On the second deal, you can save the day by leading the four of clubs instead of your trump atrocity. Declarer can win East's queen with the ace and lead a diamond, but East will win and return a club, allowing you to take two tricks in that suit. The spade king will then be the setting trick. Fortunately," I continued brightly, "I just happen to be writing a book on open-ing leads, and I'll be happy to explain . . ."

But that was as far as I got. Two of the contestants lifted me bodily, carried me to the door with great dispatch, and de-posited me carefully outside. The door closed gently, the players returned to their game, and I was left to reflect (for perhaps the thousandth time) on the peculiarities of bridge players in general and my friends in particular.

THE CHALLENGE OF THE OPENING LEAD

My approach to my friend's bridge education was a trifle injudicious; teaching should take place in books and classrooms and not at the bridge table. The errors that he made, however, *are* of extreme importance and deserve careful study. In addition to the incorrect choice of the suit to lead (which will be discussed further in later chapters), his approach to the situation was faulty. My friend regarded being on opening lead as a chore to be disposed of as quickly as possible, preferably by falling back on a handy truism. He failed to realize that opening leads are one of the most challenging and interesting aspects of the game of bridge!

If you are on opening lead, you face a situation similar to that encountered by fictional detectives such as Sherlock Holmes. You have an opportunity to assemble and evaluate various clues that are available and make deductions as to the most likely solution. Furthermore, you don't need to be a "card rack" to get in on the fun. Note that my friend, despite his miserable collection of cards, had the chance to be the hero of the hour on both of the hands that he played. To those of us who never seem to hold our fair share of the high cards, it is refreshing indeed to find an aspect of bridge that can be stimulating and enjoyable even with very bad hands!

Opening leads can be a source of immense profit (or loss) as well as entertainment. Examples of part scores, games, and even slams that have been defeated (or made) as a result of the opening lead are so frequent as to be commonplace; and the number of points won (or lost) can be enormous. On just two leads, my friend pitched 1,110 points—trick scores of 160 and 150 plus a rubber bonus of 700 scored by the opponents instead of two 50-point sets scored by his side if he makes the correct lead on both hands.

Of course, the opening lead will not be crucial on all hands that you play. Some contracts will be cold; others cannot be made, regardless of what you lead. However, unless you consistently take advantage of the opening leader's opportunity to strike the first blow for the defense, you will not win nearly as often as you should. Even when a good opening lead does not immediately defeat a contract, it is often the essential first step without which winning defense is impossible. Similarly, a poor lead will frequently place the defenders in an irretrievably bad situation.

Being a good opening leader will give you a real edge at the bridge table, for most bridge players are not nearly as good at this phase of the game as they should be. Nor is this really their fault. Many books have been written about bidding, declarer play, and defense, but it is rare to find a bridge book that devotes more than a few pages, or at best a single chapter, to opening leads, and this is simply not sufficient to allow any but the most general of ideas to be expressed. It is time for a change—time for opening leads to be given the attention due them in view of their importance and fascination.

HOW ARE *YOUR* OPENING LEADS?

This book will not teach you how to make the winning opening lead on every hand; not even top experts can do that. It will show you how to win more often, and have more fun doing it, by finding opening leads that are likely to be positively poisonous to your opponents and avoiding leads that are likely to present them with undeserved gifts.

If, like me, you are irritated beyond forbearance by the multitude of grandiose advertising claims in today's society, which the product all too often fails to live up to, you will quite properly want some documentation for the claim made in the preceding paragraph. Let's put it to the test. The problems below illustrate some of the important situations that you are likely to run into at the bridge table. Each hand, and the principle that it depicts, is discussed in a subsequent chapter in this book. All of the problems are from rubber bridge, so your primary objective is to defeat the opponents' contract, and your score is given in terms of the number of points your lead wins or loses. To simplify the scoring, we will assume that with the exception of Problem 3, neither side is vulnerable.* The problems are arranged approximately in order of increasing difficulty.

(1)	NORTH	EAST	SOUTH	WEST
	—	—	1 NT	Pass
	3 NT	Pass	Pass	Pass

* A non-vulnerable game is valued at 300 points.

You (West) hold:

♠ A 2   ♡ A 6 3   ◇ A 8 5   ♣ 6 5 4 3 2

What card do you lead?

(2)	NORTH	EAST	SOUTH	WEST
	—	—	1 NT	2 ♡
	3 ♡	Pass	3 ♠	Pass
	4 ♠	Pass	Pass	Pass

You (West) hold:

♠ 8 2   ♡ A 10 6 4 3 2   ◇ 9 7   ♣ K Q J

What card do you lead?

(3)	NORTH	EAST	SOUTH	WEST
	—	—	1 ♡	Double
	Pass	Pass	Pass	

You (West) hold:

♠ A K 10 6   ♡ 2   ◇ Q J 10 8   ♣ K Q 8 5

What card do you lead? (North-South vulnerable.)

(4)	NORTH	EAST	SOUTH	WEST
	—	—	1 ♡	Pass
	2 ◇	Pass	3 ◇	Pass
	3 ♡	Pass	4 NT	Pass
	5 ◇	Pass	6 ♡	Pass
	Pass	Pass		

You (West) hold:

♠ 10 9 8 4 3   ♡ 8 7 5   ◇ A 6   ♣ Q 6 2

What card do you lead?

(5)

NORTH	EAST	SOUTH	WEST
—	—	1 NT	Pass
3 NT	Double	Pass	Pass
Pass			

You (West) hold:

♠ 10 9 8 7   ♡ K 8 5   ◇ 9 7 6 2   ♣ 9 3

What card do you lead?

(6)

NORTH	EAST	SOUTH	WEST
—	—	1 ♡	Pass
3 ♡	Pass	4 NT	Pass
5 ♡	Pass	6 ♡	Pass
Pass	Double	Pass	Pass
Pass			

You (West) hold:

♠ 9 8 7   ♡ 6   ◇ 8 7 6 4 3 2   ♣ K Q J

What card do you lead?

(7)

NORTH	EAST	SOUTH	WEST
—	—	1 ♠	Pass
1 NT	Pass	2 ◇	Pass
2 ♠	Pass	Pass	Pass

You (West) hold:

♠ 7 5 3   ♡ 9 7 2   ◇ A J 10 2   ♣ K Q J

What card do you lead?

(8)

NORTH	EAST	SOUTH	WEST
—	—	1 ♡	Pass
2 ♣	Pass	3 ♣	Pass
3 ♡	Pass	4 ♡	Pass
Pass	Pass		

You (West) hold:

♠ 8 6 3   ♡ A K Q 2   ◇ Q 10 8 6 3   ♣ 7

What card do you lead?

(9)	NORTH	EAST	SOUTH	WEST
	—	—	1 ♠	Pass
	2 ♣	Pass	3 ♣	Pass
	3 ♡	Pass	3 ♠	Pass
	4 ♠	Pass	Pass	Pass

You (West) hold:

♠ K 4   ♡ Q J 10 9 8   ◇ K J 4   ♣ 7 3 2

What card do you lead?

(10)	NORTH	EAST	SOUTH	WEST
	—	1 ♡	1 ♠	Pass
	2 NT	Pass	4 ♠	Pass
	Pass	Pass		

You (West) hold:

♠ 5 2   ♡ Q 6 2   ◇ 8 6 3 2   ♣ 9 8 6 4

What card do you lead?

(11)	NORTH	EAST	SOUTH	WEST
	—	—	1 ♡	Pass
	1 ♠	Pass	3 NT	Pass
	Pass	Pass		

You (West) hold:

♠ K 8 3   ♡ K Q J 3 2   ◇ 10 8 5   ♣ J 7

What card do you lead?

(12)	NORTH	EAST	SOUTH	WEST
	—	—	1 ◇	Pass
	1 ♠	2 ♡	2 ♠	?

You (West) hold:

♠ A 5 3   ♡ 10 9 7 6   ◇ 4   ♣ Q J 10 8 5

What call do you make?

(13)	NORTH	EAST	SOUTH	WEST
	—	—	—	Pass
	1 ◇	Pass	1 ♠	Pass
	3 ◇	Pass	3 NT	Pass
	Pass	Pass	

You (West) hold:

♠ J 8 7 5   ♡ 8 4 3   ◇ J 4 3   ♣ A 9 6

What card do you lead?

(14)	NORTH	EAST	SOUTH	WEST
	1 ◇	Pass	2 ♣	Pass
	2 ◇	Pass	3 NT	Pass
	Pass	Pass	

You (West) hold:

♠ A K 5 2   ♡ 7 6 3   ◇ A 5 2   ♣ K 5 3

What card do you lead?

(15)	NORTH	EAST	SOUTH	WEST
	1 ♠	Pass	3 ◇	Pass
	4 ♠	Pass	4 NT	Pass
	5 ♡	Pass	5 NT	Pass
	6 ◇	Pass	7 NT	Pass
	Pass	Pass	

You (West) hold:

♠ K 6   ♡ 9 6 3   ◇ J 6 4 2   ♣ 8 7 6 3

What card do you lead?

Solutions

(1) *Three of clubs*
Score yourself: A club, +50; any other lead, —430.
This hand is discussed in Chapter 4.

(2) *King of clubs*
Score yourself: A club, +50; any other lead, —420.
See Chapter 5.

(3) *Two of hearts*
Score yourself: Heart deuce, +500; any other lead,
—160. *See* Chapter 5.

(4) *Two of clubs*
Score yourself: A club, +50; anything else, —980.
See Chapter 6.

(5) *Nine of clubs*
Score yourself: A club, +100; anything else, —550.
See Chapter 7.

(6) *Two of diamonds*
Score yourself: A diamond, +100; anything else,
—1210. *See* Chapter 7.

(7) *Five of spades*
Score yourself: A spade, +50; anything else, —110.
See Chapter 5.

(8) *Six of diamonds*
Score yourself: A diamond, +50; anything else,
—420. *See* Chapter 5.

(9) *Four of diamonds*
Score yourself: A diamond, +50; anything else,
—420. *See* Chapter 2.

(10)   *Queen of hearts*
Score yourself: Heart queen, +50; anything else, —420. *See* Chapter 5.

(11)   *Three of hearts*
Score yourself: Heart three or deuce, +50; anything else, —400. *See* Chapter 2.

(12)   *Three diamonds*
Score yourself: Three diamonds, +50; anything else, —420. *See* Chapter 8.

(13)   *Ace of clubs*
Score yourself: A club, +100; eight of hearts, —50; anything else, —430. (The heart eight should defeat the contract, but gives partner more of a chance to go wrong.) *See* Chapter 3.

(14)   *Five of spades*
Score yourself: Spade five, +50; anything else, —400. *See* Chapter 9.

(15)   *Six of spades*
Score yourself: Spade six, +100; anything else, —1520. *See* Chapter 6.

How well did you do? The maximum score is +1,400; the minimum is —8,290. As you can see, quite a bit can depend on the opening lead! Don't be distressed if you encountered some difficulty, for you will have little trouble with problems like these after you have read this book, and you will find making good opening leads enjoyable as well as profitable. Good luck!

2

Trouble over Tables

♠ ♡ ◇ ♣

There are many myths and fallacies that hold the belief of the public in spite of the fact that they are totally incorrect. For example, suppose that you are wagering with a friend over the outcome of the flip of a coin, and on the first five trials the coin falls heads up. If you are permitted to call the next toss, how should you bet? Many people would choose tails because of the "law of averages," but the correct decision is to bet on heads. If the coin is not biased in either direction, it makes no difference what you do, for your chances of winning are 50-50. If, however, the coin is flawed, the results of the previous flips strongly suggest that it is biased in favor of the head side falling face up.

A misconception that has affected most bridge players is that the important principles concerning opening leads can be summarized in a convenient table. Nothing could be further from the truth. There is nothing wrong with the idea of a table in fact, you will find one later on in this chapter), provided that its limited usefulness is made clear to the reader. A table of opening leads can serve the following functions:

(1)   The table can summarize the *card* that is most likely to be correct *once the suit has been selected*. If your fairy godmother appears at the table and advises you to lead a diamond from ◇ Q J 10 5 against the enemy's 4 ♠ contract, the table will quite correctly inform you that the proper lead is the queen. In the absence of such friendly advisors, however, it is up to you to draw the relevant inferences and deductions and decide whether or not a diamond should in fact be led, and this vital preliminary step is not (and cannot be) summarized in any table.

(2)   *All other things being equal,* the table can indicate

those holdings which are likely to make for better opening leads. Unfortunately, it happens all too often that all other things are *not* equal, and blind adherence to opening lead tables will lead to many disastrous results. For example, one maxim states that the lead from a solid sequence is highly desirable. It is entirely correct to make use of this rule in a situation such as the following:

```
                      NORTH
                      ♠ 7 5
                      ♡ 10 9 7 2
                      ◇ J 7 4
                      ♣ A K Q 2

       WEST                             EAST
       ♠ Q J 10 9 8                     ♠ 6 4 2
       ♡ A K                            ♡ 8 6 4 3
       ◇ Q 8 6 3 2                      ◇ 9
       ♣ 8                              ♣ J 9 7 5 3

                      SOUTH
                      ♠ A K 3
                      ♡ Q J 5
                      ◇ A K 10 5
                      ♣ 10 6 4
```

The bidding:

SOUTH	WEST	NORTH	EAST
1 NT	Pass	3 NT	Pass
Pass	Pass		

If West leads a diamond, South will win and attack hearts. West wins, but even if he now shifts to a spade it is too late for the defense, for South will win and drive out West's other high heart. Declarer cannot then be prevented from regaining the lead and will easily make his contract. A spade lead, however, leaves South a trick short. When West next gains the lead in whatever red suit South chooses to attack, he will knock out declarer's last spade stopper, and South cannot develop his ninth trick without allowing West to cash three spade tricks and two heart tricks.

In this situation, then, West is well advised to lead from his strong sequence, and the table cannot be faulted. But what about a hand such as the following one?

NORTH
♠ Q 8
♡ A K 6 3
♦ 9 5 3
♣ K 10 8 5

WEST
♠ K 4
♡ Q J 10 9 8
♦ K J 4
♣ 7 3 2

EAST
♠ 7 6 5 2
♡ 5 4 2
♦ A Q 8 7
♣ 9 6

SOUTH
♠ A J 10 9 3
♡ 7
♦ 10 6 2
♣ A Q J 4

The bidding:

SOUTH	WEST	NORTH	EAST
1 ♠	Pass	2 ♣	Pass
3 ♣	Pass	3 ♡	Pass
3 ♠	Pass	4 ♠	Pass
Pass	Pass		

If West is overly addicted to lead tables, he will reason (without regard to the bidding) that leading away from a king is tantamount to heresy, and that solid sequences are the key to success. He will therefore lead the heart queen, and declarer will happily win the ace, lead the king and discard a losing diamond, and finesse the spade queen. South will not mind when the finesse loses; he will simply regain the lead (after a short delay if West chooses to attack diamonds at this point), draw trumps, and run his club winners to make his game contract.

It is quite a different story if West's opening lead is a diamond. The defense will quickly cash three diamond tricks, and South will later complain about his luck when the spade finesse loses, for the contract will be defeated.

West, in fact, has no choice but a diamond, for North and South have carried on the following conversation:

SOUTH: (1 ♠) "I have an opening bid and a spade suit."

NORTH: (2 ♣) "Good! It looks like our hand. I have at least 11 points and at least four clubs."

SOUTH: (3 ♣) "I like clubs too, but don't have much else to say."

NORTH: (3 ♡) "I've got some goodies in the heart suit. How about a heart or notrump contract?"

SOUTH: (3 ♠) "I can't bid 3 NT because I don't have the unbid suit stopped, and I don't like hearts. My spades are pretty good, though."

NORTH: (4 ♠) "Well, I guess I'd better support you on my doubleton. I don't have diamonds stopped either and can't bid notrump, and 5 ♣ looks a bit too high for my taste."

SOUTH: (Pass) "Okay, let's try our luck here."

Not all of the above inferences are clear-cut—for example, North could have longer spade support on this auction—but if West is listening, he should deduce that the opponents are weak in the diamond suit. Had the bidding instead proceeded 1 ♠– 3 ♠–4 ♠, there would be no such clue, and a heart lead would then be preferable.

A suit with four top honors would be strongly endorsed by any table, but even this lead can produce bad results:

NORTH
♠ A K 8 6
♡ 5 2
◊ J 10 3 2
♣ Q J 10

WEST
♠ 7 2
♡ A K Q J 9
◊ 9 7
♣ 9 7 5 4

EAST
♠ Q 10 9 5
♡ 7
◊ A 6 5 4
♣ 8 6 3 2

SOUTH
♠ J 4 3
♡ 10 8 6 4 3
◊ K Q 8
♣ A K

The bidding:

SOUTH	WEST	NORTH	EAST
1 ♡	Pass	1 ♠	Pass
1 NT	Pass	2 NT	Pass
Pass	Pass		

West can cash four heart tricks if he likes, but declarer will simply win the next lead, drive out East's ace of diamonds, and take the rest of the tricks to make his contract. Even one heart lead will prove fatal to the defense. If, however, West leads any other suit, South is in trouble. He must attack diamonds to develop his eighth trick, and East will win the ace and shift to a heart, allowing West to cash five winners and set the hand.

The preceding hand is admittedly an extreme example, for the lead from such a strong suit will frequently prove to be successful. It is included to emphasize the fact that rigidly adhering to "rules" about opening leads is a losing policy. South's opening heart bid should alert West to the need for unusual action. South can hardly be bidding on strength in this suit—West has it all—

Typical *Card* Choices Once Suit Has Been Selected

HOLDING IN SUIT	LEAD AGAINST NOTRUMP CONTRACTS	LEAD AGAINST SUIT CONTRACTS
I TWO-CARD SUITS		
Any doubleton	Top card	Top card
II THREE-CARD SUITS		
9 8 7 or worse	Top card	Top card
J x x 10 x x Q x x Q 10 x K x x K 10 x K J x	Third best	Third best
10 9 x J 10 x Q J x Q J 10 K Q x K Q 10 K Q J	Top card	Top card
A x x A 10 x	Ace or third best	Ace
A J x A Q x	Second highest	Ace
A K x A K 10 A K J A K Q	King	King

III FOUR-CARD SUITS

Holding	Top card or fourth best	Top card or fourth best
9 8 7 6 or worse	Fourth best	Fourth best
10 x x x, 10 9 x x, J x x x, J 10 x x, Q x x x, Q 10 x x, Q J x x, K x x x, K 10 x x, K J x x	Fourth best	Fourth best
Q 10 9 x, K 10 9 x, K J 10 x	Second highest	Second highest
K Q x x, K Q 9 x, A K x x, A K 10 x	Fourth best	King
Q J 9 x, Q J 10 x, K Q 10 x, K Q J x	Top card	Top card
10 9 7 x, 10 9 8 x, J 10 8 x, J 10 9 x, A x x x, A 10 x x, A J x x, A Q x x	Fourth best	Ace
A 10 9 x, A J 10 x	Second highest	Ace
A Q J x	Ace with sure side entry; otherwise queen	Ace
A K 10 9, A K J x, A K Q x, A K Q J	King	King

IV FIVE-CARD AND LONGER SUITS

Except for the holdings shown below against *notrump* contracts, follow the same rules as for four-card suits.

10 9 7 x x	J 10 8 x x	Q 10 9 x x	K 10 9 x x	A 10 9 x x	Fourth best
				A K 10 9 x	King with sure side entry, otherwise ten
				A K J x x	King with sure side entry, otherwise fourth best
J 10 9 x x	Q J 10 x x	K J 10 x x	A J 10 x x		Fourth best *if* suit is bid by the opponents. (Otherwise, follow rules for four-card suits.)
		K Q 10 x x	A Q J x x		
		K Q J x x	A K Q x x		

But be sure to note that the following examples are different from the ones above:

Q 10 9 8 x	K 10 9 8 x	A 10 9 8 x			Second highest
	K J 10 9 x	A J 10 9 x			
10 9 8 7 x	J 10 9 8 x	Q J 9 8 x	K Q 10 9 x	A K J 10 x	Top card
		Q J 10 8 x	K Q J 9 x		
		Q J 10 9 x	K Q J 10 x		

V TRUMP LEADS

K Q, Q J, J 10, 10 9, any doubleton including the ace	Top card
Any other doubleton; J 10 x	Lowest card
9 8 7 or worse, 10 x x, 10 9 x	Middle card
A x x, A 10 x, A J x, A Q x	Ace or third best
Other three-card holdings	Generally, follow rules for three-card suits

so he should have some length to make up for this deficiency. If West assumes the role of detective and draws this deduction, he will realize the necessity for leading a different suit and allowing partner to play hearts through declarer. Granted, South does not have to have the heart ten, but since he has more hearts than either North or East he is certainly more likely to have this critical card. What if East cannot win a trick? Then North and South must be cold for at least two notrump regardless of what West leads.

There are many clues of this sort that you can deduce, and this is what gives opening leads their fascinating properties. As we will see later, the clues may come from the opponents' bidding, partner's bidding, or the cards in your hand (all thirteen of them, not just the ones in the suit you are considering for your lead). Of course, you should not look for a wildly unusual lead on every hand; extremism in refusing to follow the table is as much of a vice as is blind adherence to the table. Before attempting to polish up your detective work, however, you should first have a good understanding of what card to lead once you have chosen a suit, and in this respect a table can be of assistance. However, since attempting to memorize large batches of information without comprehending the underlying principles is a poor way to learn anything (and not very pleasant, either), let's take a look at both the table and the reason for some of the more important entries.

Note: To avoid making the table even larger than it now is, "x" is used to represent any card below a ten. Sometimes, however, the presence of a nine, eight, or seven will affect the choice of the card to lead, so be careful to consult the most relevant holding. For example, from Q 10 7 2, lead the 2 (see Q 10 x x), but from Q 10 9 5, lead the 10 (see Q 10 9 x). From Q J 9 2 or Q J 9 8, lead the queen (see Q J 9 x, the only relevant holding listed).

CHOOSING THE CARD TO LEAD

The card that you select for your opening lead serves two

important functions. The first and most obvious of these is to help pave the way for the eventual defeat of the contract (insofar as this is possible). The second purpose, which is equally important, is to give your partner information about your holding in the suit, so that his defense (including both his play to the first trick and his actions at a later point) will be as accurate as possible. The opening lead table has been designed with these objectives in mind. It cannot, of course, give you the right answer on all hands, for unusual situations do arise from time to time which require unusual action. More often than not, however, the choice of card indicated by the table will be the correct one.

To see how the two objectives are in fact accomplished by the leads recommended by the table, let's consider some of the suggested leads in detail.

Leads from Doubletons

If you choose to lead from a suit in which you hold two small cards, such as 7 3, the choice of card will probably have little effect insofar as the trick-taking situation is concerned because there are so many higher cards outstanding. Thus, the main consideration is to give information to your partner. To help him distinguish doubletons from longer suits, you should lead the top card. When you next follow suit with a lower card, partner will be alerted to the possibility that you may have only two cards in the suit. With a relatively long suit, you will often want to save your intermediate spots until later, when partner may well be out of the suit and you will have to fight on alone as best you can. Thus, a reasonable strategy (and one followed by most players) is to lead the top card from short suits of no particular value and to lead low from long suits.

Leading the top card from a doubleton is likely to help the trick-taking situation as well when you have an honor in the suit. For example:

DUMMY
♠ K 9 5

YOU   PARTNER
♠ Q 6   ♠ A J 10 7 4

DECLARER
♠ 8 3 2

If you decide to lead this suit (perhaps because partner has bid it) and choose the six, the defense is in serious difficulty. If dummy plays low, partner can win with the ten but will be unable to continue the suit without presenting the opponents with a trick. Even if dummy's king is put up, the defense may have trouble getting untangled. Partner will win with the ace, but your queen will take the next trick, and partner will need an entry in a side suit in order to be able to gain the lead and cash a third spade trick. The lead of the queen, however, resolves all problems. If dummy ducks, you remain on lead to press the attack through the king; and if dummy's king is played, partner can quickly run three spade tricks.

Leads from Three-Card Suits

Experts disagree on the lead from three small cards, such as 8 4 2. The most widely used method, which is generally regarded as standard, is to lead the top card.* This will cause some confusion inasmuch as partner may think you have a doubleton, but perfect communication on opening leads is not possible, and the top card serves the valuable function of informing partner that you do not have an honor in the suit. The following example shows how the lead of the top card can help partner resolve a difficult problem:

* Alternative methods will be discussed in the Appendix.

NORTH
♠ A K Q J
♡ Q 6 3
◇ 7 4 3
♣ 10 5 3

WEST   EAST
♠ 8 4 3 2   ♠ 10 9 6 5
♡ 9 5 2   ♡ 7 4
◇ A Q 6   ◇ J 10 9 2
♣ 8 4 2   ♣ A 9 6

SOUTH
♠ 7
♡ A K J 10 8
◇ K 8 5
♣ K Q J 7

South is playing a 4 ♡ contract, and since North has bid
spades, West elects to lead a club. If he leads the eight, East will
reason that he should look elsewhere for tricks—and quickly,
what with dummy's spade suit leering at him as a potential park-
ing place for declarer's side-suit losers. East will therefore win
the first trick with the ace of clubs and switch to the jack of
diamonds, allowing the defenders to score three diamond tricks
and defeat the contract. On any other return, declarer can pitch
all his diamonds on dummy's spades and make *six* hearts.

Perhaps you think that East should defend the same way
even if West leads the deuce of clubs. This in not necessarily true,
as the following layout shows:

NORTH
♠ A K Q J
♡ Q 6 3
◇ 7 4 3
♣ 10 5 3

WEST
♠ 8 4 3 2
♡ 9 5
◇ A 6 5
♣ K J 4 2

EAST
♠ 10 9 6 5
♡ 7 4
◇ J 10 9 2
♣ A 9 6

SOUTH
♠ 7
♡ A K J 10 8 2
◇ K Q 8
♣ Q 8 7

Again South is playing 4 ♡, and West leads the deuce of clubs. If East wins and shifts to the jack of diamonds, South covers with the king and must now make his contract; the defenders cannot take more than three tricks before allowing declarer to regain the lead and discard his losers on dummy's spades. If, however, East wins with the club ace and returns a club,* West will cash two more club winners and quickly lay down the ace of diamonds to defeat the contract.

To be sure, East will not always be able to reach the correct decision in such situations. In the first example, West *could* hold ♣ K J 8 and the ace (but not the queen) of diamonds, in which case a club return is necessary to defeat the contract. No opening lead method will win on all occasions (otherwise there would not be disagreement as to the best method to use), but the eight is very unlikely to be West's lowest club. Similarly, in the second example, West might hold the ace and queen of diamonds and the king (but not the jack) of clubs, which would make a diamond shift essential to beat the contract. Yet West would lead a low club because he holds an honor in the suit. More often than not,

---

* The *nine,* to show no more than two remaining clubs. With an original holding of four or more clubs, East would return his fourth best.

however, knowing whether West has an honor in the suit he has led will help East reach a winning decision.

Incidentally, you should help partner distinguish between a doubleton and tripleton on your second play of the suit you lead. If you lead the eight from 8 4 2, follow with the four the next time the suit is played. Thus, when your second play is the lowest outstanding spot, partner will know that your original holding was a doubleton; if you lead the eight and follow with the deuce, your original holding must have been 8 2.

As the table indicates, the lead of a small card from a three-card holding shows an honor in the suit led. However, don't lead small when you hold two *touching* honors in the suit. Holdings such as

K Q 3   Q J 5   J 10 7   or 10 9 4

are strong enough so that you can afford the lead of an honor, and the customary practice is to lead the top one. An exception occurs in the case of A K 3, from which the king is led. The argument favoring this play is that it enables partner to distinguish between an unsupported ace and an ace-king combination.* Also, underleading an ace against a suit contract runs the risk that if either declarer or dummy has a singleton in this suit, your ace will be ruffed away later and your side may lose the trick that it deserves. Even when this danger fails to materialize, the underlead of an ace against a suit contract is so unusual that partner may be misled and make a costly error. Therefore, the underlead of an ace should be reserved for extreme emergencies.

Leads from Four-Card Suits

With four small cards, you have a choice of leads. If you lead your lowest card and partner can tell that you do not have an honor in the suit (perhaps because he can see all of them in his hand and dummy), he will know that you have at least four

---

* This method entails the disadvantage that the king is led from both ace-king and king-queen, and partner may not be able to ascertain your holding when it is critical to do so. Lead methods designed to resolve this difficulty are discussed in the Appendix.

cards in the suit, for you would lead the top card from a shorter suit. This can be helpful in situations such as the following:

DUMMY
◇ Q J 8 6

YOU   PARTNER
◇ 9 5 4 2   ◇ A K 10 7

DECLARER
◇ 3

Suppose that declarer is playing a 6 ♠ contract. If you lead the deuce of diamonds and dummy's queen is played, partner will win with the king and shift suits, for the lead of the deuce marks you with four cards and declarer with a singleton. (Your deuce could be a singleton, but partner can usually tell from the bidding and the rest of the hand whether you have one or four cards in a suit.) If you lead the nine, partner might be tempted to try to beat the slam by leading a second round of diamonds; declarer would ruff and obtain a possibly useful discard on dummy's remaining high diamond.

Unfortunately, matters are rarely this simple. If you lead a low card and partner cannot see all the honors in the suit, he may assume that you have one (or more) of them and lead the suit back when a switch would be preferable. The situation is similar to that involving three-card holdings discussed previously, where the lead of a top card warned partner against continuing the suit. As a result, the table cannot decide this issue for you, and each case will have to be judged on its merits. If it is more important to give partner the count, lead small; if it is more important to tell him that your holding in the suit is far from robust, lead the highest. (Some experts lead the second-highest, on the theory that the top card may be high enough to win a trick later on if it is not squandered on the first trick.) We will look at some examples in subsequent chapters.

With four to an honor, or four to two honors lacking a solid or nearly solid sequence, the lead of a low card is usually best. A possible exception occurs in the case of Q J 4 2; the lead of the queen against suit contracts is often recommended. However, the suggested lead of a small card is superior in many situations:

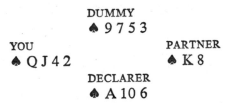

                        DUMMY
                        ♠ 9 7 5 3
        YOU   PARTNER
        ♠ Q J 4 2   ♠ K 8
                        DECLARER
                        ♠ A 10 6

Partner cannot afford to unblock the king on the lead of the queen, and so must play small. Declarer wins the ace, and the suit is blocked. Leading small allows the defenders to ensure two quick tricks in the suit if you have just one side entry. The whole hand might be:

                        NORTH
                        ♠ 9 7 5 3
                        ♡ Q 7 4 2
                        ◇ K Q J
                        ♣ Q J

        WEST   EAST
        ♠ Q J 4 2   ♠ K 8
        ♡ 10 3   ♡ 9 8
        ◇ A 9 5 2   ◇ 8 6 4 3
        ♣ 8 7 4   ♣ A 10 9 6 5

                        SOUTH
                        ♠ A 10 6
                        ♡ A K J 6 5
                        ◇ 10 7
                        ♣ K 3 2

Playing in 4 ♡, South will win the queen of spades lead with the ace, draw trumps, and drive out the ace of diamonds. West can lead a spade to East's king, but cannot regain the lead, and South is able to make his contract by pitching his losing spade on a high diamond. A low spade lead, on the other hand, defeats the contract with little difficulty. East's king drives out South's ace, and West can cash two spade tricks upon gaining entry with the diamond ace. East's ace of clubs will then provide the setting trick.

The lead of a low card from this combination will also work well if partner has a doubleton ten. If partner has either the king or ten, or both, with length, it probably makes little difference what card you lead. The low card may cost when partner holds the ace-ten behind dummy's king, but against that must be set the gain from this situation:

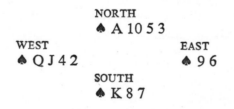

NORTH
♠ A 10 5 3

WEST
♠ Q J 4 2

EAST
♠ 9 6

SOUTH
♠ K 8 7

If West leads the queen, South wins the king and finesses the ten the next time, brightly informing everyone that West's lead of the queen shows the jack—irritating the defenders considerably. After the lead of a small card, South will probably play low from dummy, either out of carelessness or because he is playing West for queen-nine or jack-nine of spades, and be the one who is irritated by the result.

Holdings such as

Q 10 9 2   K J 10 3   K 10 9 5   and A J 10 3

involve what are called *interior sequences*. Here the lead of the second-highest card, namely the top one of the interior sequence, is likely to be helpful:

NORTH
♠ J 7 4

WEST   EAST
♠ Q 10 9 5   ♠ K 3 2

SOUTH
♠ A 8 6

If West leads the five and dummy plays small, East must put up the king, and declarer gets two tricks in the suit. Exchange South's eight with East's three and East may still put up the king for fear of giving South a quick and possibly undeserved trick. (Against notrump, West could have ♠ A Q 9 5.) If West leads the ten, however, East has much less of a problem.*

As in the case of three-card suits, the top card is led from solid or nearly solid sequences (except that the king is led from ace-king combinations). *But be sure the combination is nearly solid.* The reason for leading the jack from a holding such as J 10 9 6 is to prevent declarer from winning an undeserved trick with the eight-spot or partner wasting a king or ace on a collection of deuces and treys. With J 10 4 2, however, an honor lead is likely to be losing strategy. If you drive out the higher honors in this way, you will be left with a four and a deuce as two-thirds of your assets. This is unlikely to produce further enrichment in the way of trick-taking! It is better to lead small and let partner help attack the enemy's strength, reserving your limited honor strength for later on in the battle. If partner can provide no help in this suit, then any card is probably doomed to defeat.

Holding K Q 8 6, however, you should lead the king against suit contracts. The king lead will quickly establish at least one trick for your side even if declarer has the ace (provided neither declarer nor dummy has a singleton). Sooner or later, declarer or dummy will be able to ruff, so you had better get your trick while you can. Similarly, with holdings involving the ace-king, lead the

---

* He may still be uncertain whether the jack or ten lead is West's highest card or the top of an interior sequence. See the Appendix for conventional treatments designed to resolve this difficulty.

king against suit contracts rather than a small card. Declarer will gloat in a most obnoxious fashion if he wins an undeserved trick after a small-card lead and later ruffs away your ace or king (or both), and you should be careful to prevent such a glaring display of bad manners (and lost defensive tricks).

Leads from Five-Card and Longer Suits

Against suit contracts, principles similar to the case of four-card suits apply to five-card and longer suits. With five small cards, lead the fourth-best if your objective is to give partner the count. When you next play your smallest card, he will know that your original holding was five cards. With a holding such as 9 8 6 4 3 2, lead the four and follow with the three (again assuming your goal is to give partner information about your length); he will notice that the deuce is missing and calculate your length accordingly. (If he is the sort of player who will not notice that the deuce is missing, you might as well lead anything; but follow the suggested procedure anyway to stay in practice until you get a respectable partner.) On the other hand, if you feel that it is more important to tell partner that you have no high cards in this suit, lead the highest (or, possibly, the second-highest). With one honor or broken holdings involving two honors, lead your fourth-best card; with solid or nearly solid sequences, lead the top card (but lead the king from ace-king combinations); with interior sequences, lead your second highest card (top of the interior sequence). If you are going to lead from a suit such as K Q 4 3 2, it is even more important than before to lead the king, so as to set up a trick before declarer or dummy can ruff. The more cards you have in the suit, the fewer cards the opponents can have, and the more imminent is the danger of a ruff. For the same reason, you should also lead the queen from Q J 8 6 5 4 and the jack from J 10 6 5 3 2 rather than fourth-best.

Against notrump contracts, however, things are different. Here, your main goal is to develop tricks by length. Declarer cannot ruff anything; thus, any time you lead a suit that all the other players are out of, the trick will belong to you. If your suit is not a solid one, you will need some help from partner. Since you are long in the suit, he is likely to be short, so it is especially important to lead small from most holdings so as to avoid clashing your honors on the same trick and turning declarer's losing spots into winners. Therefore, as the table shows, you need quite a solid suit before you can deviate from the usual fourth-best lead.

When a suit is bid by an opponent, this is usually a sign that he holds at least four cards in the suit. (Artificial bids, such as responses to Blackwood, are not included in this category.) Particularly when the suit is bid on your right (i.e., by declarer), you usually should lead fourth-best against notrump contracts even from some very strong holdings. For example, suppose declarer has bid spades in the following situation (obviously, before you had a chance to do so):

```
                    DUMMY
                    ♠ 6 4
        YOU                     PARTNER
    ♠ A K Q 5 3                 ♠ J 7
                    DECLARER
                    ♠ 10 9 8 2
```

Leading the king blocks the suit; a low card allows you to run the first five tricks. Exchange partner's jack for one of declarer's lower cards, and the low lead is still correct, for it establishes a fourth trick in the suit while retaining a spade in partner's hand. This is likely to be essential unless you have a sure side entry.

Similarly, with ♡ K Q J 3 2, you should lead the three if the suit is bid on your right. (Remember, we are assuming that you have decided to lead this suit, and the only question is the best card to select.) This can win in several ways:

```
                    DUMMY
                    ♡ 9 5
        YOU                     PARTNER
    ♡ K Q J 3 2                 ♡ 10 7
                    DECLARER
                    ♡ A 8 6 4
```

Here, the lead of a low heart is essential to avoid blocking the suit. Even if the positions of the nine and ten are switched, a low heart is still best; declarer may not realize that it cannot be wrong to put up dummy's ten and may hold himself to one trick (and one stopper) in the suit by playing the five.

```
                         NORTH
                         ♠ J 9 5 4 2
                         ♡ 5 4
                         ◇ Q J 7
                         ♣ Q 8 6
        WEST                             EAST
        ♠ K 8 3                          ♠ A 7
        ♡ K Q J 3 2                      ♡ 7 6
        ◇ 10 8 5                         ◇ 9 6 4 3
        ♣ J 7                            ♣ 10 9 5 4 2
                         SOUTH
                         ♠ Q 10 6
                         ♡ A 10 9 8
                         ◇ A K 2
                         ♣ A K 3
```

The bidding:

SOUTH	WEST	NORTH	EAST
1 ♡	Pass	1 ♠	Pass
3 NT	Pass	Pass	Pass

A 4 ♠ contract would be better, but only superb defense will defeat 3 NT. If West leads the heart king, South ducks, and the defense disintegrates. West can continue with the queen, but South simply wins with the ace and attacks spades. West lacks enough entries both to set up his suit and run it, and East, who is out of hearts, can only sit by helplessly and watch. Now suppose West's opening lead is the heart three. Declarer may chuckle temporarily as he wins a cheap trick with the eight, but his joy will be short-lived. If his declarer play is particularly sharp, South

will cross to dummy with a diamond or club and play a spade,
attempting to catch East in a midday nap. East should quickly
put up his ace and return a heart, however, and South's last heart
stopper is knocked out while West retains the spade king as an
entry. Since South cannot get a ninth trick without at least some
help from the spade suit, the contract is defeated by one trick, and
the last chuckle belongs to the defenders.

Note that if hearts had not been bid, and West had no reason
to suspect a four-card holding in either the North or the South
hand, it would be reasonable to lead the king to guard against
declarer and dummy having the ace and ten between them with
no more than three cards in either hand.

Similar good things can happen in the following situations:

	DUMMY	
	♠ K 3	
YOU		PARTNER
♠ Q J 10 5 4		♠ A 6
	DECLARER	
	♠ 9 8 7 2	

Declarer has bid spades—and some nerve he has, too, with
such a weak suit. The lead of the spade queen ensures a stopper
for declarer, who simply covers with the king; after the lead of a
small spade, declarer will probably put up dummy's king (the
correct play, if you have the ace) and the defense will take the
first five tricks.

	DUMMY	
	♠ Q 4	
YOU		PARTNER
♠ J 10 9 6 3		♠ K 5
	DECLARER	
	♠ A 8 7 2	

This time declarer's spade bid is more reasonable, but he will still get an extra stopper if you lead the jack. After the lead of the six, only a clairvoyant could refrain from putting on dummy's queen, and declarer is held to one spade trick.

Similar considerations apply to the other holdings listed for which the recommended lead is fourth-best *if* the opponents have bid the suit, and you can work these out for yourself given the clue of the previous examples. However, a word of caution is in order. The lead of the fourth-best card from a holding containing three honors can easily lose a trick if neither declarer nor dummy has four cards in the suit, for the opponents may then win a truly undeserved trick with a low spot. *Don't* let the following happen to you:

                         DUMMY
                         ♠ K 4 3
        YOU   PARTNER
        ♠ Q J 10 5 2   ♠ A 8 7
                         DECLARER
                         ♠ 9 6

If you lead the five and dummy plays small, declarer must get a trick in the suit; the lead of the queen prevents him from enjoying even a single spade winner.

                         DUMMY
                         ♠ K 4 3
        YOU   PARTNER
        ♠ Q J 10 5 2   ♠ 8 7
                         DECLARER
                         ♠ A 9 6

Now the lead of the five gives declarer three tricks, where he should get only two—as he will if you lead the queen.

DUMMY
♠ Q 5 2

YOU   PARTNER
♠ J 10 9 6 3   ♠ K 7 4

DECLARER
♠ A 8

The lead of the six gives declarer two tricks if he plays small from dummy; the jack lead restricts him to a single winner.

Do you see the difference in principle between these hands and the earlier examples? Here, your fourth-best card is a winner by length, since no opponent holds more than three cards in the suit. By the time you get around to playing it, everyone will be out of your suit, and your low card will win. Therefore, it is pointless to risk having the opponents win an undeserved trick by leading a low card. But when an opponent has bid the suit and is likely to have four cards in it, your fourth-best card will run into competition from the opponent's length; it will not have an uncontested run at the trick after three rounds of the suit have been played, but will still have an opponent's card to beat. Therefore, unless your own fourth-best card is very high, it is better to gamble on finding help from partner—or on declarer's making a mistake. You will not always know whether or not an opponent has a four-card suit; he may bid a three-card suit or conceal a four-card suit to fool you (or because he doesn't know any better). At times, you will simply have to guess. Even so, you will come out ahead far more often than the player who blindly leads an honor card by rote.

Of course, by all means lead the top of your sequence (or the top of an interior sequence) when it is powerful enough to withstand even a four-card suit in the hands of an opponent, such as

Q J 9 8 5   Q J 10 9 2   K J 10 9 4   K Q 10 9 6

and so on. The critical matter here is that your fourth-best spot is in relatively little danger of being beaten out by one of the opponents' cards, so you can be aggressive and blast away with your honors. Also, keep in mind your objectives in any given hand. I once saw a player make the absolutely abominable lead of the four of diamonds against an opposing notrump contract from

♠ 8 6   ♡ A 7 3   ◇ K Q 8 4 2   ♣ 9 7 4

Does my vehemence surprise you? Excuse me! I forgot to mention that the contract was *six* notrump! The four of diamonds would have been a good choice against a 3 NT contract barring some strong indication to the contrary (such as a heart bid by partner, or a couple of diamond bids by an opponent), but against 6 NT you need only two tricks to defeat the contract, not five. The obviously correct lead is the diamond king; if declarer needs even one heart trick for his contract, you will be able to swoop in with your ace and cash the diamond queen to beat the slam. Similarly, if the opponents get to a *four*-notrump contract, lead the king of clubs from:

♠ 7 5 3   ♡ 8 4   ◇ A K 2   ♣ K Q J 3 2

even if clubs are bid by the opponents.

A discussion of every one of the entries in the table would be hopelessly tedious; fortunately, it is also unnecessary. If you keep in mind the general principles that we have discussed, you should be able to work out the rationale underlying any of the other situations that you may run into. A special word is in order, however, regarding the lead from A K J 10 3 against notrump. Even if you are not overly addicted to conventions, I strongly advise you to use the lead of an ace against a notrump contract, if obviously from a long suit, to ask partner to play an honor if he has one, and to signal his count (play a high spot from an even number, and a low spot from an odd number) if he lacks an honor. This simple device can bring you in a bushel of points when the indicated combination comes up, and it works as follows:

                    DUMMY
                    ◇ 8 6 5
        YOU   PARTNER
        ◇ A K J 10 3   ?
                    DECLARER
                       ?

You lead the ace, partner plays the seven, and declarer
follows with the four. Partner cannot have the queen or else he
would have played it in response to your request. The high spot
shows an even number of diamonds. (A singleton is unlikely
since the deuce is missing; unless declarer is false-carding, partner
has it.) Partner cannot have four diamonds (otherwise declarer's
low card played on the first trick would be his only one, and partner would have the queen), so he has at most two. Consequently,
you know that declarer's queen will not drop on the next round of
diamonds. Declarer's actual holding is ◇ Q 9 4, and a second
diamond lead from you will give him an undeserved trick with the
queen.

                    DUMMY
                    ◇ 8 6 5
        YOU   PARTNER
        ◇ A K J 10 3   ?

                    DECLARER
                       ?

When you lead the ace this time, partner plays the deuce and
declarer the four. Unless the deuce is singleton, partner is showing
an odd number of cards, clearly three in this case, and you can
play your king with reasonable confidence that you will drop declarer's queen and be able to run the whole suit. (If partner's
deuce is a singleton, there is no point waiting for him to get on
lead, since he cannot lead any more diamonds unless he borrows
one from another deck, and a diamond continuation by you will
be right most of the time anyway.) Declarer's holding is ◇ Q 4,

and he is hoping desperately that you will shift to another suit.

Clearly, if you lead the ace and partner drops the queen, all problems are resolved, and you simply cash your winners.

Playing this little convention can prevent some serious headaches, and costs practically nothing. Just be sure not to lead an ace from a long suit unless you are willing to have partner drop his honor on the trick. Also, partner should exercise a modicum of discretion. If you lead the ace of diamonds and he holds ♢ K 9 8 6 4, he should reason that you are probably trying to hit his suit from a short holding such as A 7 3 and simply signal with the nine. Usually, the dummy and the bidding will make it quite clear to him whether you are leading a short or a long suit. By the way, you should discuss this convention with your partner prior to the game, so that he will know what is expected of him.

Trump Leads

The proper plays when leading trumps are summarized briefly in the table. The general ideas are as follows: With a small doubleton, leading the lowest card preserves the higher spot for a possible overruff of declarer later on. With three small cards, leading the middle one followed by the smallest one again preserves the highest spot for a possible overruff, and gives partner the message that you have a third trump (since you did not lead your lowest one). This may prove particularly helpful if he has to decide whether or not you can ruff a side suit later on; his play for a ruff will not be notably successful if you are out of trumps. With J 10 3, lead *small*. Partner is likely to have a singleton, since the opponents do not choose a trump suit on an equitable basis but selfishly pick the one in which they have a great many cards. Leading the jack will cost a trick in various situations, such as:

DUMMY
♡ K 9 4 2

YOU   PARTNER
♡ J 10 3   ♡ Q

DECLARER
♡ A 8 7 6 5

DUMMY
♡ Q 6 5 2

YOU   PARTNER
♡ J 10 3   ♡ K

DECLARER
♡ A 9 8 7 4

In either case, if you lead the jack, declarer can pick up the whole suit without a loss by simply playing low from dummy, capturing partner's honor with his ace, and finessing against your ten on the next lead. Leading the three-spot ensures that your side will get the trick it deserves.

HOW DO YOU LEAD?

This is a serious question! If you recall the second disaster that befell my friend in the previous chapter, you'll remember that he did everything but send up a flare to alert declarer to the fact that he had a problem. He hesitated, fidgeted, grimaced, and made his discomfort evident to everyone but some people watching television several blocks away. Defense is difficult enough without going out of your way to tip off declarer when you have an uncertain choice (or an obvious one). And the declarer is the only one who will benefit, for it is unethical for your partner to draw inferences from the slowness or speed of your play. Here's an example of how declarer can benefit from your indecision:

DUMMY
♠ 9 8 2
♡ Q 6 4
♦ J 10 6
♣ A K 10 3

DECLARER
♠ K 7 3
♡ K J 3
◇ A K Q 3 2
♣ J 7

Declarer opens 1 NT, and is raised to 3 NT by his partner. West leads the spade five, dummy plays low, and East's jack drives out declarer's king. South can count eight top tricks, and has two lines of play. He can lead a heart and allow the opponents to take their ace, and if spades are divided 4-3 the defenders can cash only three additional tricks before surrendering the lead. However, this play will fail if spades are 5-2, for the defenders will cash enough spade tricks to set the contract. Alternatively, declarer can try the club finesse. If it wins, he will have nine tricks; but if it fails he will certainly be set, for even if the spades are 4-3 the defenders will win one club trick, three spade tricks, and the heart ace. South cannot determine West's spade length from the opening lead; West could have ♠ A 10 6 5 4 or ♠ A 10 6 5, for example.

It is far from clear as to what play to choose, and an unwary West may give the show away. If West holds a hand such as

♠ A 10 6 5   ♡ A 9 8 5   ◇ 7 5   ♣ 9 8 6

and agonizes for several moments before his opening lead, declarer may well choose to play him for a four-card spade suit, attack hearts, and make his contract. After all, West would not have nearly so much of a problem with five spades to the ace, which would be a much more obvious choice.

Since it is also unethical to hesitate with no problem so as to fool declarer, the obvious solution is to try and maintain the same tempo for every lead that you make. Even with an obvious choice, take a moment or two before leading; also, try to do some of your thinking during the bidding so as to avoid long hesitations after the auction has ended. Don't give declarer any information to which he's not entitled!

Review Quiz

Here's a short quiz to help you check your understanding of the principles discussed in this chapter. In each case, assume that you have decided to lead the suit shown, and select your card for each of the conditions given.

	YOU HOLD:		WHAT IS YOUR LEAD AGAINST:
(1)	Q 10 8 6 4 3	(a)	a notrump contract?
		(b)	a suit contract?
(2)	A K	(a)	a suit contract?
(3)	9 5 3	(a)	a notrump contract?
		(b)	a suit contract?
		(c)	a suit contract if this suit is trumps?
(4)	Q 10 9 8 5	(a)	a notrump contract if this suit is bid on your right?
		(b)	a suit contract?
(5)	Q J 9 6	(a)	a notrump contract?
		(b)	a suit contract?
(6)	K 10 3	(a)	a notrump contract?
		(b)	a suit contract?
(7)	6 3	(a)	a notrump contract?
		(b)	a suit contract?
		(c)	a suit contract if this suit is trumps?
(8)	K J 10 6	(a)	a notrump contract?
		(b)	a suit contract?

(9)   J 10 9 5 3   (a)   a notrump contract?
                          (b)   a suit contract?

(10) K Q 6 2   (a)   a notrump contract?
                          (b)   a suit contract?

(11) A K 8 5 3   (a)   a notrump contract?
                          (b)   a suit contract?

(12) 10 9 6 3   (a)   a notrump contract?
                          (b)   a suit contract?

(13) A K Q 10 8 4   (a)   a notrump contract?
                          (b)   a suit contract?

(14) Q J 10 5 3   (a)   a notrump contract if this suit
                                is bid on your right?
                          (b)   a suit contract?

(15) K J 8 5 3   (a)   a notrump contract?
                          (b)   a suit contract?

(16) A Q 8 4   (a)   a notrump contract?
                          (b)   a suit contract?

(17) J 10 2   (a)   a notrump contract?
                          (b)   a suit contract?
                          (c)   a suit contract if this suit is
                                trumps?

(18) A J 10 6 4   (a)   a notrump contract if this suit
                                is bid on your right?
                          (b)   a suit contract?

(19) 9 6 5 2   (a)   a notrump contract?
                          (b)   a suit contract?

(20) Q 9 8 3   (a)   a notrump contract?
                          (b)   a suit contract?

Solutions

(1)   (a) *The six* The next time you play a low card, you
      will play the four. Since you led your fourth-best card and

have now played a lower one, you must have started with at least five; and if partner notes that the three has not been played, he should correctly ascertain your length.

(b) *The six*   The reasoning is the same against a suit contract.

(2)   (a) *The ace*   Lead the top card from any non-trump doubleton. When you next play the king, partner should be able to discern why you deviated from the usual rule of leading king from ace-king.

(3)   (a) and (b) *The nine*   Lead the top card from three small.

(c) *The five*   Preserve the nine for possible overruff duty. When you follow with the three, partner will know that you have a third trump.

(4)   (a) and (b) *The ten*   This suit is strong enough to lead the top of the interior sequence at any contract, even if declarer has bid the suit.

(5)   (a) and (b) *The queen*   Lead the top card of your nearly solid sequence.

(6)   (a) and (b) *The three*   Lead low from three to one honor, or two honors that do not form a sequence.

(7)   (a) and (b) *The six*   Lead the top card from any non-trump doubleton.

(c) *The three*   When leading trumps, lead small from a low doubleton.

(8)   (a) and (b) *The jack*   Lead the top of an interior sequence.

(9)   (a) *The jack*   If you have a strong hunch that declarer has four cards in this suit, however, the five could be the winning play.

(b) *The jack*   No choice against a suit contract; declarer or dummy will undoubtedly ruff long before the fourth round is played, so length-winners are almost certainly of no concern.

(10)   (a) *The deuce*

(b) *The king*   Set up a probable winner while you can.

(11)   (a) *The five*   The usual fourth-best lead, hoping to take a few length-winners later in addition to the ace and king.

(b) *The king*   Declarer's ruffing power argues against

risking the loss of the first trick in an attempt to develop length-winners.

(12)   (a) and (b) *The three*   This is not a strong enough suit to lead the ten-spot.

(13)   (a) *The ace*   Get partner to clarify the issue by playing the jack if he has it or by signaling his length so that you can tell whether or not you should try to drop the jack if it is in declarer's hand.

(b) *The king*   Standard from ace-king combinations.

(14)   (a) *The five*   With the suit bid by declarer, this is much more likcly to be the best lead than is the queen.

(b) *The queen*   Once again, you should not lead a small one against a suit contract, for an opponent will ruff sooner or later (probably sooner).

(15)   (a) and (b) *The five,* your fourth-best card.

(16)   (a) *The four*

(b) *The ace*   Except for emergencies, don't underlead aces against suit contracts.

(17)   (a) and (b) *The jack*   With a three-card suit, lead the top of two touching honors (always excluding the infamous ace-king).

(c) *The deuce*   In the trump suit, there is too much danger of blowing a trick if you lead the jack; partner may have a singleton honor.

(18)   (a) *The six*   Had the suit not been bid, you would lead the jack.

(b) *The ace*   If you are going to lead this suit, it is better not to underlead an ace (if only to preserve partnership harmony for the future).

(19)   (a) and (b) *The answer depends on your objectives*   To give partner the count, lead the deuce; to indicate the lack of an honor in the suit, lead the nine or six.

(20)   (a) and (b) *The three*   Nine-eight is not treated as an interior sequence.

3

Gathering the Evidence

♠ ♡ ◇ ♣

Had Sherlock Holmes chosen to become a serious student of
the game of bridge, he undoubtedly would have been a superb
opening leader. Holmes trained himself to take greater notice of
what he saw than the average person did, and mastered the
technique of drawing accurate deductions from his observations.
Thus, for example, it was no secret that the dog did nothing in the
nighttime, but only Holmes took note of the importance of this
fact and deduced that the intruder was known to the animal. And
it was apparent to anyone who cared to look that the steps to
Dr. Watson's office were more worn than the neighboring steps to
an alternative office Watson might have purchased, but only the
famous detective took careful note of this fact and deduced that
Watson had bought the better practice—the office more frequently visited by patients.

The deductions that can be drawn by the opening leader are
just as interesting, yet usually not as difficult as the ones that kept
Holmes in business. Yet, like Dr. Watson, most bridge players
fail to take note of the available clues. While this detective work
is important at all stages of the defense, it is vital to success at
opening leads. This is, obviously, because you have less information at your disposal before you lead than at any other time
during the defense. You know only (1) the bidding, (2) the
strength of your hand, and (3) the strength of the suit you are
considering for your lead.

CLUES FROM THE BIDDING

Like newspapers, some auctions are more informative than others. Some of the kinds of clues that you can get from the bidding are:

Weak spots in the opponents' hands: The opponents may point out their own Achilles heel by steadfastly refusing to bid a certain suit or notrump. However, be careful not to be misled by auctions such as the following:

NORTH	EAST	SOUTH	WEST
1 ♠	Pass	2 ♣	Pass
2 ♦	Pass	3 NT	Pass
Pass	Pass		

Although no one has bid hearts, the jump from 2 ♦ to 3 NT shows that South is more than willing to commit the hand to notrump, and he should therefore have strength in the unbid suit. Hearts may nevertheless be the right lead, but the defenders should not expect to have a field day right at the start. If, on the other hand, an opponent bids notrump with apparent reluctance, or refuses to bid notrump at all, the unbid suit may well be only lightly protected:

NORTH	EAST	SOUTH	WEST
1 ♦	Pass	1 ♥	Pass
1 ♠	Pass	3 ♦	Pass
3 ♥	Pass	3 ♠	Pass
3 NT	Pass	Pass	Pass

North's heart support can hardly be awesome, or he would have driven the hand to 4 ♥; the same applies to South's spade support. Yet neither North nor South was bursting with eagerness to rush into a notrump contract. The chances are that both of them are somewhat displeased about the club situation, a fact East will do well to note when considering his opening lead.

NORTH	EAST	SOUTH	WEST
1 ◇	Pass	1 ♠	Pass
2 ◇	Pass	3 ◇	Pass
3 ♡	Pass	3 ♠	Pass
4 ◇	Pass	Pass	Pass

Here the club situation is likely to be even more appalling insofar as North and South are concerned, or else they might have tried 3 NT rather than settling for a diamond partial.

Strong spots in the opponents' hands: If an opponent has a particularly strong suit, he is likely to inform his partner of this fact by rebidding it, or possibly jumping in it. Similarly, if you bid a suit and your left-hand opponent makes several attempts to wind up in a notrump contract, you have a valuable clue as to where the missing strength in your suit is likely to be. For example:

NORTH	EAST	SOUTH	WEST (you)
1 ◇	Pass	1 ♡	1 ♠
1 NT	Pass	3 ♣	Pass
3 NT	Pass	4 ♣	Pass
4 ♡	Pass	Pass	Pass

North must be well heeled in spades to try so hard for a notrump contract after your overcall. If your spade suit is very strong, a spade lead may be right anyway, but suppose you hold:

♠ K J 10 9 3   ♡ Q 10 5   ◇ Q J 10   ♣ K 4

You should not be at all surprised to find North with the ace and queen of spades, and you have an attractive alternative lead—the queen of diamonds. The whole hand might well be:

NORTH
♠ A Q 8 6
♡ A 7
♢ K 8 6 5
♣ Q 8 3

WEST
♠ K J 10 9 3
♡ Q 10 5
♢ Q J 10
♣ K 4

EAST
♠ 7 5 4 2
♡ 6 3
♢ A 9 3 2
♣ 9 7 2

SOUTH
♠ —
♡ K J 9 8 4 2
♢ 7 4
♣ A J 10 6 5

A spade lead allows South to make five hearts (he has nothing to lose by putting in dummy's queen, for even in the unlikely event that East has the king South can simply ruff, cross to the heart ace, and discard a diamond on the spade ace). A diamond lead, however, gives the defenders two diamond tricks immediately, and West must eventually score a heart and a club trick to defeat the contract. Of course, the hand may be cold with any lead, but you should not be concerned with that possibility; winning opening leads are rarely found by players adopting such a pessimistic outlook.

The opponents' distribution: South's bidding on the previous hand gives an excellent clue as to his distribution. He bid clubs twice, and so should have at least five; he bid hearts before clubs, so his hearts should be at least as long. South must be very short in diamonds and spades, and there is therefore a very real danger that he will discard losing diamonds on North's spades. What about the reverse possibility—that he wishes to discard losing spades on dummy's diamonds? If this is the case, then West is probably helpless, for with North marked with the ace and queen of spades on the bidding West cannot set up any spade winners fast enough to prevent the discards.

You will often find valuable clues as to the opponents' distribution from their bidding. A player who rebids a suit should have at least five cards in it; a player who bids three suits is likely to be short in the fourth suit; and so on. You should acquire the habit of forming a picture of the opponents' hands while the bidding is going on; you will not always be right, but the more you try, the better you'll do!

The opponents' general strength: If the opponents stagger into game after a relatively unaggressive auction, the chances are that they have little extra strength over the 26 points needed for game (and they may even be a little short). For example:

NORTH	EAST	SOUTH	WEST
1 ◇	Pass	1 ♠	Pass
2 ♠	Pass	2 NT	Pass
3 NT	Pass	Pass	Pass

North's single spade raise shows a minimum or near-minimum opening; South was not strong enough to bid game directly but could muster up only a 2 NT bid (which North could pass); and North scraped up a raise to game. Clearly, the opponents have little strength in reserve, and therefore it may not be imperative for your side to set up tricks quickly. As a contrasting example, consider the straightforward auction 1 NT–3 NT. The opening bidder shows a maximum of 18 points, so his partner knows that slam should not be bid even if he has as many as 14 points, for the total of 33 points needed to bid slam will not be present. Thus, on this auction, the opponents could have quite a bit of extra strength in spite of the fact that neither one made a try for slam. If so, you may have to attack quickly, as declarer can possibly set up enough winners to make his contract—given time.

Partner's best suits and relative strength: If your partner bids a suit, the chances are that he has at least some values in it. Most players realize this, but fewer are aware of the implications of partner's failing to bid:

NORTH	EAST (partner)	SOUTH	WEST (you)
1 ♡	Pass	1 NT	Pass
Pass	Pass		

East cannot have a good spade suit of five or more cards, or else he would have overcalled 1 ♠, and leading a spade from a worthless doubleton or tripleton in an attempt to hit your partner's suit is unlikely to be successful. (He might, however, have a respectable club or diamond suit which is not strong enough for an overcall at the *two* level.)

Your partner's defensive strength is often indicated by his bid. If he makes a takeout double, you can expect him to have some helpful defensive values; if he makes a preemptive bid, you should not base your lead strategy on the hope of finding him with high-card strength in the side suits. Just as with the opponents' bidding, you should form a mental picture of partner's hand any time he assists you by entering the bidding.

A Cautionary Note

Perhaps you've heard of the poor fellow who got a tip on a stock from a friend, bought a few thousand shares, and watched glumly as the stock plummeted downward. A few months later, he received another tip from the same friend, invested heavily again, and again lost a considerable sum. This sad pattern was repeated several times, and one day the chap found himself recounting his difficulties to the friendly official at the neighborhood loan company. When asked why he persisted in taking his investment advice from such a dubious source, he replied, "He's the only person I know who has inside knowledge about the stock market"!

If you are enjoying an evening of rubber bridge, you will have ample opportunity to observe the bidding habits of the other players. If it becomes apparent that the opponents are bidding with more enthusiasm than skill, you should reject any but the most obvious of inferences, even though the opponents are the only ones with inside information about their hands. If, for example, you see that they fail to bid some of their five-card suits, rebid four-card suits, bid notrump without stoppers in your suit, fail to reach cold games with 31 high-card points, don't support partner with four cards in his suit, and so on, any message you get from their bidding can only be regarded as highly suspect. Similarly, if you see that your partner likes to overcall on very sketchy suits, keep this fact in mind and don't be quite so willing to lead the suit that he has bid. Paradoxically, good opponents can sometimes be easier to play against than poor ones—or at least to lead against—because their bidding is likely to be more trustworthy. The good detective knows when he runs into "red herrings"; insist on bona fide, grade-A quality clues, and if you cannot get them from the opponents' or your partner's bidding, limit yourself to more reliable sources of information—the cards in your hand.

CLUES FROM THE STRENGTH OF YOUR HAND

If your opponents bid a game and you have 13 or 14 high-card points, it is quite reasonable to deduce that partner is probably broke. The opponents may be counted on for approximately 26 points, and while some of these may be in distributional values rather than high cards if they are playing a suit contract, there is still very little left over for partner to have. You can only enrich the opponents by planning your lead on the assumption that partner can contribute some high-card help if the strength of your hand indicates that he cannot possibly supply it. Similarly, if the opponents stop in game and you have a Yarborough, partner can be counted on for some values. The opponents may have somewhat more than the 26 points needed for game, but they cannot have all the points or else they would have headed on toward slam. In this situation, partner may well be fairly strong and may be counting on you to cooperate with him in setting up his winners, and he will have a perfect right to be annoyed if you adopt a defeatist policy and lead the nearest card because your hand is weak. Besides, opening leads are fun even with bad hands, and after all that passing during the bidding some entertainment should be a welcome change, so take advantage of it.

A second type of clue that you can draw from the strength

of your hand is whether or not your side is likely to be in trouble.
If dummy has bid and rebid a suit and you are on lead and happen to hold K J 3 in that suit, desperate measures may be called
for. Any finesses in this suit are likely to win, for the strength will
be to your left, and you may have to set up tricks in a hurry.
Furthermore, if declarer is playing a suit contract and has indicated shortness in the suit, he will have a relatively easy time
ruffing out your high cards because of your lack of length. The
whole suit might be distributed as follows:

DUMMY
♡ A Q 8 6 5

YOU   PARTNER
♡ K J 3   ♡ 10 7 2

DECLARER
♡ 9 4

Once declarer gains the lead, he can finesse the heart queen,
cash the ace, and ruff a third round, exhausting your side of
hearts and establishing two heart winners in dummy for discards
of side-suit losers.

It is also a bad sign if you hold four or five very small cards
in a suit in which dummy has promised length, and declarer is
playing a suit contract. In Chapter 1, my friend failed to appreciate the significance of this clue in the following situation:

DUMMY
◊ K Q J 9 8 6

MY FRIEND   EAST
◊ 5 4 3 2   ◊ A 10

SOUTH
◊ 7

Dummy had bid and jump-rebid diamonds, indicating a
probable six-card suit. Assuming that South has at least a sin-

gleton, one lead plus one ruff will establish the whole suit for declarer no matter how you arrange the high cards in the dummy and East hands.

If, however, declarer is marked with shortness in dummy's side suit and you are also short (for example, you have a worthless doubleton), then partner may have some unpleasant surprises in store for declarer and you are less likely to need to collect your tricks in other suits in a hurry. Similarly, it is a fairly reassuring state of affairs if you hold strength and length in a suit that your right-hand opponent has bid, and a sign of possible trouble if your holding is weak (such as three or four very small cards) in one of your right-hand opponent's side suits.

Thus, in addition to obtaining a clue as to the strength of partner's hand from *how strong* your own hand is, you can also draw useful inferences from *where* your strength is placed— whether declarer is likely to be pleasantly or unpleasantly surprised by the location of your high cards.

CLUES FROM THE STRENGTH OF YOUR SUIT

The kind of deduction that you can make from a specific suit is a more obvious one, but is nevertheless worth repeating: it is perfectly reasonable to lead your strongest suit when "all other things are equal." Lacking clues to the contrary from either the bidding or the general strength of your hand, you would prefer to lead from Q 10 8 6 than Q 4 3 2 because the former suit has more powerful intermediate cards and needs less help from partner to set up tricks. Similarly, you would prefer a solid sequence such as J 10 9 8 to either of the above two holdings. Where most players go wrong is that they use the strength of their suits as the only factor in reaching a decision as to what to lead, and ignore the valuable information that can be drawn from other sources.

SUMMARY: TWO ILLUSTRATIVE EXAMPLES

In subsequent chapters, you will find numerous examples of how the principles described above are put into practice by the

opening leader. For now, let's conclude this general discussion
with two examples that show how the various principles are used
in combination to arrive at the lead that is most likely to be a
winner.

In Chapter 1, we saw that a trump lead from

♠ 7 4   ♡ 9 6 5 2   ◇ 5 4 3 2   ♣ K 10 4

was somewhat less than successful after the auction

WEST	NORTH	EAST	SOUTH
Pass	1 ◇	Pass	1 ♠
Pass	3 ◇	Pass	3 ♠
Pass	4 ♠	Pass	Pass
Pass			

How should West have reasoned? Let's look at each of the possible sources of information.

The bidding: North has a long and strong diamond suit,
probably six cards in length since he jumped in it. He also has a
powerful hand, as indicated by his jump rebid. There are two
unbid suits, hearts and clubs, and either might be a weak spot in
the enemy's armor.

West's general strength: West has only three high-card
points, yet the opponents have stopped short of slam. Therefore,
East should have a fair amount of high-card strength. The
diamond situation represents a potential disaster; as we have seen,
South will be able to establish the suit for discards very quickly
if he has at least a singleton diamond. Therefore, West cannot
afford a passive trump lead.

The strength of West's suits: Having concluded that it is
necessary to build tricks in a hurry, West should decide to lead
one of the unbid suits. Either hearts or clubs could be right, but
East will need quite a lot of heart strength for the defenders to
cash enough tricks in that suit to defeat the contract. In clubs,
however, West's king is a valuable contribution that will help the

trick-taking potential of the defense, and the ten-spot is a potentially important second honor that may prove very useful; less help is needed from partner if the attack is made on clubs rather than hearts. On this reasoning, West should lead the four of clubs.

The hero of the next hand was British expert Ralph Swimer. The hand was reported by Terence Reese in the September 1964 *Bridge World*. Swimer held

♠ J 8 7 5   ♡ 8 4 3   ◊ J 4 3   ♣ A 9 6

and heard the following bidding:

WEST (Swimer)	NORTH	EAST	SOUTH
Pass	1 ◊	Pass	1 ♠
Pass	3 ◊	Pass	3 NT
Pass	Pass	Pass	

The following clues were available:

The bidding: First of all, North has shown a good hand and a long diamond suit. The defense could have a diamond stopper as East might have an honor in the suit, but there is a fairly good chance that the diamonds will run and that the defenders may have to take their tricks in a hurry. Second, South has bid spades and is likely to be fairly well off in that suit. Third, partner had a chance to overcall hearts at the one-level and failed to do so, and he is therefore unlikely to have a good heart suit. He might, however, have a respectable club holding, as a *two*-level overcall requires more strength than a one-level overcall and East may have had to pass even with fair club values.

West's general strength: West has only six high-card points and the opponents have stopped in 3 NT. Therefore, partner is likely to have some high-card values.

West's suit strength: In clubs, West can make a powerful contribution to the trick-taking potential of the defense with his ace; in hearts, partner will have to carry on alone.

The lead from three to an ace against a notrump contract is not often recommended, but after assembling all the evidence a club lead would seem to be the master stroke. Swimer did in fact lead the ace of clubs, and the whole hand was:

NORTH
♠ A
♡ Q J 6
♢ K Q 10 9 8 6 2
♣ Q 2

WEST (Swimer)
♠ J 8 7 5
♡ 8 4 3
♢ J 4 3
♣ A 9 6

EAST
♠ 4 3 2
♡ A 10 9 2
♢ 7
♣ K J 8 7 4

SOUTH
♠ K Q 10 9 6
♡ K 7 5
♢ A 5
♣ 10 5 3

The very fine club lead was highly successful, and the contract went down two. To be sure, a heart lead to East's ace followed by a club switch would have achieved the same result. (Real life does not always reward virtue in the form of the one best opening lead.) However, East might not have found the club switch; and South could easily have held the heart ace instead of the king, in which case only the club lead would beat the contract. The goal of the opening leader is to find the lead *most likely* to result in the ultimate defeat of the contract, as Swimer did in this example.

4

Leads Against Notrump Contracts

♠ ♡ ◇ ♣

Declarers, like Ebenezer Scrooge, are not noted for philan-
thropy. If one of them contracts for game in notrump, it is probable that his side holds the balance of high-card power and he
expects to score a handsome profit so long as there are no trumps
and the defense is unable to ruff away his winners. After all, had
distribution rather than honor cards been the main asset for his
side, he probably would have opted for a suit contract; and had
the high cards been distributed more evenly between your side
and the opposition, he would not have bid all the way to game.
Consequently, you can be fairly certain that your attempt to defeat the contract will be hindered by a marked deficiency in high-
card strength.

This is unquestionably a regrettable state of affairs, and you
would indeed be at a crippling disadvantage were high cards the
only method for taking tricks against a notrump contract. Fortunately, it is often possible for you to hoist declarer by his own
petard and turn his lack of a trump suit into an advantage for
your side. If no handy petard is available, your long suits will do
admirably as a substitute to bring about the downfall of evil,
inequity, and declarer. Remember, you have an important advantage in that you have the opening lead—the chance to strike the
first blow in the battle to develop tricks. For example, we saw in
Chapter 2 that holding

♠ Q J 10 9 8   ♡ A K   ◇ Q 8 6 3 2   ♣ 8

West was able to build enough tricks to defeat the contract provided that he led a spade, thus putting time on the side of the

defenders by immediately knocking out one of declarer's two spade stoppers. When West regained the lead with a heart, he forced out declarer's last spade stopper while still holding a high heart as an entry. With any other lead, the time factor would work for declarer, who could drive out West's two high hearts before his two spade stoppers were dislodged. Thus, despite the fact that the declarer's side holds more than twice as many points as the defenders', the spade length plus the ability to play first provides the equalizer—*if* West makes the right opening lead.

A similar situation with even smaller spots doing yeoman work arises in the following example:

NORTH
♠ J 10 6
♡ K Q 5
♢ K J 9 7
♣ Q 10 9

WEST
♠ A 2
♡ A 6 3
♢ A 8 5
♣ 6 5 4 3 2

EAST
♠ 9 8 7 5 3
♡ 10 9 7 4
♢ 4 2
♣ 8 7

SOUTH
♠ K Q 4
♡ J 8 2
♢ Q 10 6 3
♣ A K J

The bidding:

SOUTH	WEST	NORTH	EAST
1 NT	Pass	3 NT	Pass
Pass	Pass		

East and West are faced with a disheartening 28-to-12–point deficit in the high-card department. They will prevail, however, if West makes good use of his opportunity to develop winning tricks by leading a club (the three-spot). South wins the first trick and plays diamonds; West takes his ace and leads another club. South wins in his hand and attempts to sneak through the critical trick by playing a low spade, hoping that West will duck (in which case South will have one spade trick in the bag and will switch to hearts and make his contract). West goes right up with the spade ace and drives out South's last club stopper, and the contract is doomed. Declarer has only eight tricks and must try hearts, whereupon West takes his ace and plays his remaining two lowly clubs—the only clubs left in the game.

If West squanders the opportunity to get a head start by leading any other suit, South will make his contract with an overtrick, for West will be one fatal step behind in his attempt to drive out declarer's club stoppers before his own aces have been eliminated. Having thrown away his time advantage, West will find in the end that he will have to throw away his potential club winners on declarer's established tricks—much to the defenders' dismay and declarer's profit—instead of having the fun of watching declarer sluff his winners on West's good clubs.

Thus, like Clark Kent rushing off to the nearest telephone booth to change himself into Superman (and with considerably less commotion), your meek and unassuming low cards can be transformed into powerful trick-taking winners. The much-abused rule about leading "fourth from your longest and strongest suit" was designed with this fact in mind. Like anything else, however, the rule will work against you if it is used excessively. Your longest and strongest suit is certainly a reasonable place to look for potential winners, but there may be important clues which indicate that your side should seek out other sources for taking tricks. Your partner also has thirteen cards to contribute to the defense, and your best suit may well not be the one that is strongest when the combined partnership assets are considered. Therefore, let us deal with the questions of *when* it is desirable to follow the "fourth-best" rule, and why the *fourth*-best card is the one that is usually recommended.

ENTRIES

In order to take tricks with length-winners, you obviously must be able to get back into your hand to lead them. Therefore, leading fourth-best from your longest suit is likely to be winning strategy only if you possess high cards, either in your suit or in the side suits. In the previous example in this chapter, West was correct to follow the fourth-best rule because he held probable entries that would allow him to cash the length winners that he established.

If your hand is dismally short of entries, you should not give up on the idea of establishing length-winners—but your strategy should be to build up the length-potential in *partner's* hand since your poverty-stricken collection indicates that *he* is likely to have the necessary entries. This is admittedly harder to do than setting up your own suit, but it is better to make an attempt to find partner's defensive "weapons" than to lead your own suit with no entries. When you do try to hit partner's suit, avoid leading a singleton. A holding such as three small spots makes it less likely that the opponents have great length in the suit and thus partner has a better chance to develop length-winners. Some examples:

(a)	♠ 8 6 3	(b)	♠ 10 9 2
	♡ A J 9 6 5		♡ 7 6 5 4 2
	◇ 7 4		◇ 6 4 3
	♣ 6 5 3		♣ 9 7

In each case, your right-hand opponent opens 1 NT and is raised to 3 NT by his partner. With hand (a), you should lead the six of hearts. Since you have only five high-card points, partner is likely to take some tricks in the side suits, and when he returns hearts your ace (and possibly the jack as well) will enable you to gain the lead and play more hearts. Holding hand (b), you should not lead from your long heart suit, for you have no entries and will never be able to cash the hearts even in the unlikely event that the suit becomes established. Try to help partner by hitting *his* suit; since there is no indication which one it is, lead the spade ten, choosing the suit in which you can offer the most help. (Also, as we will see later, an *unbid major* is often the best suit in which to try and hit your partner.) The importance of keeping entries until the critical moment explains the vacillation of the table in Chapter 2 concerning the lead from certain holdings against notrump contracts. For example, suppose that you are on lead after the auction 1 NT–3 NT with each of the following hands:

	(a)		(b)
	♠ A 3		♠ 6 3
	♡ 8 5 3		♡ 8 5 3
	◇ A K 10 9 5		◇ A K 10 9 5
	♣ 7 4 2		♣ 7 4 2

With hand (a), lead the king of diamonds and try to drop a singleton or doubleton jack or queen in an opponent's hand. Unless one opponent has ◇ Q J 3 2 (in which case you are probably doomed to defeat regardless of what you lead, since partner is unlikely to have an entry in view of your strength), you will be able to run the diamonds when you regain the lead with the ace of spades. Holding hand (b), however, it is essential to retain the high diamonds to use as entries after the suit has been established. Lead the ten of diamonds; in view of your length in the suit, partner may have only a doubleton and you should try to leave him with one to play back. The whole suit may be distributed as follows:

DUMMY
◇ J 7 4

YOU   PARTNER
◇ A K 10 9 5   ◇ 6 2

DECLARER
◇ Q 8 3

Lead the ten and you will be able to run four tricks when partner gains the lead and returns a diamond; lead the king and you will take only two diamond tricks. The ten lead is also best if dummy's four of diamonds is moved to declarer's hand. If declarer wins the first trick in either hand, you will be able to run the suit the next time partner leads it. Declarer can prevent this by ducking the first trick in both hands, but must pay the price of giving you a third diamond trick in the process.

SUIT LENGTH

The knowledgeable opening leader perceives a considerable difference between four-card and five-card suits, and is by no means equally content about leading from either one. Broken four-card suits are fairly poor places to look to develop winners. Holding A K 6 3, for example, you have two certain tricks against a notrump contract, and that's all—unless the cards break perfectly or partner is also long in the suit, neither possibility being very likely. Consequently, it will usually be inadvisable to waste your opening defensive blow by leading the three-spot in an attempt to establish the six. Even leading from a three-card suit may be preferable, since the odds are better that partner may be long in that suit.

Now consider what happens when you lead from a five-card suit, such as A K 9 6 3 or A Q 9 6 3. Your lead of the six gives you a good chance of setting up two length-winners, the nine and the three. When you hold five cards in a suit, it will happen a fair amount of the time that neither declarer nor dummy holds more than three cards. Thus, you may well be able to take four tricks in this suit right after the opening lead has been made, and declarer will have good reason to be frightened.

There is one important exception to the reverence usually accorded five-card suits as compared to four-card suits. A solid or nearly solid four-card suit, such as Q J 10 8 or K Q 10 7, is a good place to start the attack, since you will probably be able to overpower the enemy's lower spot-cards even if one of them has four cards in the suit. Such a four-card suit is preferable to a weak five-card suit.

You will not as often hold six-card and longer suits, but when you do you should be enthusiastic about leading them, for there is great potential for developing length-winners and the opponents are less likely to interfere by being long in the suit. However, entries (either in your long suit or the side suits, and preferably at least one of the latter) are essential, for partner is probably very short in your suit and you will have to gain the lead a few times, first to set up your long suit and finally to cash the established winners.

PASSIVE LEADS

At times you will be faced with a rather dreary choice where most leads are unpleasant. An example would be:

♠ 8 6   ♡ A Q 5 3   ◇ K J 3   ♣ J 7 4 2

Against a 3 NT contract, you should avoid the heart or club lead; *four*-card suits headed by the ace-queen or by the lone jack are usually poor choices for the reasons already discussed. The diamond lead is not likely to establish any length-winners and may easily lose a trick if declarer has the ace-queen, so by elimination the eight of spades is the best choice. You are not so much trying to hit partner with a good suit (not that you would mind, but you have quite a few high cards and cannot expect him to have much) as you are trying to avoid giving declarer a gift on the opening lead. With a *five*-card suit, a gift on the first trick may prove to be a sound investment by establishing several length-winners, but with a four-card suit you are likely to reap little return because your assets are too meager.

The discussion of the preceding few pages can be summarized in the following principles for leading against notrump contracts when the bidding provides no clues:

(1)   With a poor hand lacking entries, try and hit your partner's long suit.

(2)   With a moderate or good hand, develop your suits that have favorable holdings (such as five or more cards, or a nearly solid four cards). If your own suits are unattractive (such as A Q 4 2, for example), make the safest possible lead.

Needless to say, the bidding will often play an important role in the choice of lead. For now, however, let's look at some examples where the auction has been an uninspired 1 NT–3 NT, and you are on lead. Quiz yourself by selecting your lead in each case before consulting the answers.

Problems

(a)	♠ 8 6	♡ K J 8 6 3	◇ A 10 4 2	♣ 7 3
(b)	♠ A Q 8 6	♡ J 10 9 5	◇ 6 5 3	♣ 10 4
(c)	♠ 7 4 3	♡ 8 7 6 5 4 2	◇ 8 3	♣ 10 3
(d)	♠ Q J 10 9	♡ Q 8 6 5 3	◇ 7 3	♣ 6 4
(e)	♠ J 7 6 3	♡ 8 6 5	◇ A Q 10 5	♣ K 3
(f)	♠ Q 10 8 3	♡ A 7 3	◇ A 8 4	♣ A 6 2
(g)	♠ K 7	♡ Q 7 3	◇ K 9 8 6 3	♣ 8 4 3
(h)	♠ K 4 2	♡ Q 10 9 8 3	◇ 10 9 4	♣ 8 6
(i)	♠ K J 2	♡ K 10 3	◇ 7 6 3 2	♣ K 10 3
(j)	♠ 7	♡ K 6	◇ 7 5 4 3 2	♣ 8 6 5 4 2
(k)	♠ A K 10 9 4	♡ 7 3	◇ 8 6 5	♣ J 3 2

Solutions

(a) *Six of hearts* An ideal hand on which to follow the rule of "fourth from your longest and strongest suit": probable entries with the diamond ace and heart honors, a five-card suit, and no strong indication to the contrary from the bidding.

(b) *Jack of hearts* A nearly solid four-card suit is a good place to look for tricks.

(c) *Seven of spades* There is no future in the hearts, as you are very unlikely to be able to cash them even if they become established.

(d) *Queen of spades* The one time a four-card suit is preferred to a longer suit is when the four-card suit is solid or nearly solid and the longer suit is weak.

(e) *Eight of hearts* Leading one of the other suits has too much to lose and too little to gain in the way of setting up winning tricks. Go passive.

(f) *Three of spades* With just about all of the outstanding high cards, you cannot expect much help from partner. He may have the spade jack, however, and if he doesn't the contract is probably cold anyway.

(g) *Six of diamonds* The side honors may well provide entries with which to press the attack in your longest suit.

(h) *Ten of hearts* Don't forget to lead the top of an interior sequence. Your hand is somewhat shy of entries, but the spade king is a likely possibility, and the heart suit is good and may well be established quickly.

(i) *Seven of diamonds* The holdings in the other three suits are too unappetizing to lead from. You may lead either the top card or fourth-best from four small cards, and the seven is selected here to suggest to partner that you are not overly eager to have diamonds returned and that a shift to another suit is definitely worth considering.

(j) *King of hearts* You should be willing to make an unorthodox lead when all the signs point to it. You do not have enough entries to warrant an attack on the very weak minor suits, and your lack of high cards suggests that partner is probably well off in that department. Therefore, you should try to hit partner's suit, and hearts should be preferred to spades because you have something to contribute in hearts (the king and a second card in the suit) while partner will have to do all the work if you choose spades.* Always lead the top from a doubleton; a low heart lead might well block the suit.

(k) *Ten of spades* With a sure side entry, you would lead the spade king.

CLUES FROM THE BIDDING

No self-respecting spy who wandered into the neighborhood cafeteria for lunch and happened to sit next to two enemy scien-

---

* As we will see in Chapter 7, partner would double 3 NT with a solid or nearly solid five-card or longer spade suit and a sure side entry, which is another reason for preferring the heart lead.

tists discussing classified information would concentrate on his spaghetti instead of the secret data. Nor should you fail to note any communications that the opponents exchange during the bidding, for their efforts to paint accurate pictures of their hands so as to arrive at the best contract will often provide clues as to the best opening lead.

An opponent is likely to have some length and probably some strength in a suit that he bids, and not be quite so well off in a suit that he fails to mention. Consequently, an unbid suit often represents a good place to begin the attack. This is not as likely to be true in the case of an unbid *minor* suit, because it is much easier to make game by taking nine tricks at notrump than it is to take eleven tricks with a minor suit as trumps; thus, an opponent may well choose to proceed directly to notrump without bothering to bid a minor suit. Major suit games, however, are more frequently desirable and it is less often correct for a player to suppress a good major suit, so an unbid *major* is more likely to be a potential weak spot. Let's look at some examples:

	NORTH	SOUTH	YOU (WEST) HOLD:
(a)	1 ♠	2 ♡	♠ Q 10 7 5 ♡ Q 10 8 6 ◇ J 3
	3 ◇	3 NT	♣ J 10 4
	Pass		
(b)	—	1 ♡	♠ Q 4 3 2 ♡ Q 10 8 2 ◇ 7 3
	2 ◇	2 NT	♣ K J 5
	3 NT	Pass	
(c)	1 ♠	2 NT	♠ A 5 ♡ 10 9 8 ◇ J 7 6 3
	3 ♡	3 NT	♣ J 5 4 2
	Pass		

In hand (a), each opponent has promised at least four cards (and possibly more) in the suits he has bid. A lead from one of your major suits would be reasonable were the suit not bid by the enemy, but on the given auction you should revise your plans and lead the jack of clubs. There is not enough potential gain for your side to risk helping declarer set up one of the suits his side had bid by leading it.

In hand (b), your ordinary lead would be the heart deuce, choosing the stronger of your two four-card suits. South has bid hearts, however, and may welcome a lead up to his strength and length. Attempt to foil him by leading the two of spades.

In hand (c), South has not bid either of the minor suits directly, but his willingness to play in notrump and refusal to support either of North's major suits strongly suggests that he is very well off in clubs or in diamonds. The lead from four to a jack is usually an unattractive one, and having deduced that South has good values in the minors you should lead the ten of hearts.

It is by no means always best to avoid the lead of a suit bid by the opponents. Whether or not you should be deterred from leading your best suit depends on whether your assets justify an attack on the enemy's home grounds:

(a)	♠ 8 6 3	(b)	♠ Q J 10 9 3	(c)	♠ J 10 3 2
	♡ A K 3		♡ K 8 3		♡ Q 5
	◇ K J 10 5 3		◇ 7 3		◇ J 10 8 7
	♣ 8 6		♣ J 4 2		♣ K J 6

The bidding:

SOUTH	WEST (you)	NORTH	EAST
1 ◇	Pass	1 ♠	Pass
1 NT	Pass	3 NT	Pass
Pass	Pass		

In hand (a), you have two potential entries in hearts and good intermediate diamond spots. If partner has as little in diamonds as the nine, your best strategy may well be to give declarer two early tricks with the ace and queen so as to set up three for yourself before the heart honors are driven out. Lead the five of diamonds (not the jack, which would be correct had the suit not been bid by the opponents).

In hand (b), your spade suit is so strong that you can probably establish tricks on power even though North has bid the suit. The heart king is a potential entry, but even if your hand proves to be entryless the spade lead has the additional advantage of being most unlikely to give anything away. Lead the queen of spades.

Hand (c) is very unappetizing and you should be happy simply to avoid giving declarer an undeserved gift on the first trick. The nearly solid diamond sequence offers the most safety, so lead the jack of diamonds. You have too much high-card strength to warrant an all-out attempt to hit partner's suit, and the holdings in the unbid suits suggest that you are more likely to give away a trick than to build up any eventual winners if you choose to lead them.

In addition to highlighting potential weak and strong spots, the opponents' auction (plus the other clues at your disposal) may alert you to the need for taking tricks in a hurry. Suppose that you hold:

♠ 10 9 8 7   ♡ Q 8   ◇ Q 8 6   ♣ 6 5 3 2

A spade lead against a notrump contract would certainly seem to be reasonable; it is unlikely to give anything away, and may build up a trick or two, because of your solid sequence. But suppose the bidding proceeds as follows:

SOUTH	WEST (you)	NORTH	EAST
1 ♣	Pass	1 ♠	Pass
3 ♣	Pass	3 ♡	Pass
3 NT	Pass	Pass	Pass

Now you cannot afford to lead a spade; it is unlikely to give away a trick, but it may well cost the contract. South has shown a fine club suit, and you can tell from your poor club holding that he will be able to establish it with little difficulty. In addition, the bidding suggests that diamonds may be the enemy's weak point. Therefore, you should lead the six of diamonds. If South has this suit well stopped, he will probably be able to make the contract regardless of what you lead; you must hope that the full hand is something like the following:

NORTH
♠ A 6 5 4 2
♡ K 6 5 3 2
◇ 4 2
♣ 7

WEST
♠ 10 9 8 7
♡ Q 8
◇ Q 8 6
♣ 6 5 3 2

EAST
♠ Q J
♡ J 9 7 4
◇ K J 9 7 3
♣ A 8

SOUTH
♠ K 3
♡ A 10
◇ A 10 5
♣ K Q J 10 9 4

With any lead but a diamond, South has time to knock out the club ace and will easily make his contract. In general, you should tend to get active—try and take tricks quickly—when the opponents' bidding is full of vim and vigor, and when you suspect that the cards are favorably placed for declarer. Tend to select a passive lead if the opponents struggle into game or if you think the cards are lying badly for declarer, for he may need all the help he can get to fulfill his contract.

If the opponents' bidding indicates that the strength is concentrated in one hand, special measures may be called for. For example:

(a)

SOUTH	WEST (you)	NORTH	EAST
1 NT	Pass	3 NT	Pass
Pass	Pass		

(b)

SOUTH	WEST (you)	NORTH	EAST
—	—	1 ◇	Pass
1 NT	Pass	3 NT	Pass
Pass	Pass		

You (West) hold:

♠ A Q 10 5 3   ♡ 7 6 2   ◇ 8 5 3   ♣ 8 4

Given auction (a), lead the five of spades. South is marked with a strong hand, and the suit may well be distributed as follows:

DUMMY
♠ J 7 4

YOU
♠ A Q 10 5 3

PARTNER
♠ 9 6

DECLARER
♠ K 8 2

With auction (b), however, lead the queen of spades. South has shown about 6 to 9 points and North approximately 20 points, so the king is more likely to be with North. The queen lead will reap handsome dividends if the suit is distributed as follows:

DUMMY
♠ K 7 4

YOU
♠ A Q 10 5 3

PARTNER
♠ 9 6

DECLARER
♠ J 8 2

Here, the normal lead of a low spade would give declarer two tricks (and two stoppers) in the suit.

A potential source of clues from the bidding will frequently be at your disposal when the opponents play the Stayman convention. After an opening 1 NT bid, a 2 ♣ Stayman response is artificial (promising nothing about the club suit) and asks opener to bid his four-card major suit if he has one and 2 ◇ if he does not. He may not pass. (Almost all experienced players use some form of this convention, and are required by bridge law to make it known before the game.) In such cases, close attention to the bidding can be helpful in deciding on your opening lead. What can you deduce from the following auctions?

(a)	OPENER	RESPONDER	(b)	OPENER	RESPONDER
	1 NT	2 ♣		1 NT	2 ♣
	2 ♡	3 NT		2 ◇	3 NT
	Pass			Pass	

(c)	OPENER	RESPONDER
	1 NT	3 NT
	Pass	

In exhibit (a), Responder bids 2 ♣ to inquire about a possible four-card major in Opener's hand, and Opener proudly announces possession of a four-card heart suit. Responder does not seem particularly excited about this development, however, and contracts for game in notrump. Unless his Stayman response was psychic (a poor strategy avoided by most players), the only reason Responder can have had for not bidding 3 NT at his first turn was that he holds a four-card spade suit and was hoping that Opener would respond 2 ♠ (or bid 4 ♠ over Responder's subsequent 3 NT bid). Therefore, the opening leader should act just as though Responder had bid spades. For example, lead the five of diamonds, not a spade, from

♠ Q 10 8 2   ♡ 6 4 3   ◇ Q 10 7 5   ♣ A 7

Since the 2 ♣ response is artificial and does not show a club suit, do not be dissuaded from a normal club lead if you have one. Similar reasoning applies to an artificial 2 ◇ response by Opener. The 2 ♣ bid simply says, "Do you have a four-card major?" and the 2 ◇ reply says, "No; sorry about that."

In example (b), Responder is marked with at least one four-card major suit. However, Opener has denied possession of a four-card major suit and is therefore likely to be well off in the minors. Consequently, your best play when in doubt is to try and guess which four-card major Responder does *not* hold and lead that.

Example (c) looks trivial on the surface but can provide a clue to the resourceful opening leader. If the opponents are playing the Stayman convention, it is reasonable to conclude that Responder does not hold a four-card major suit (else he might well have chosen to respond 2 ♣). Of course, Opener may have a four-card major, but there is at least some indication that a major-suit lead may strike oil, and this can often help resolve a close decision. Back in Chapter 1, my friend encountered the problem of what to lead on this auction holding

♠ 10 9 6   ♡ J 8 6 3 2   ◊ 10 9 8   ♣ 7 4

He was so relieved that the opponents stopped short of slam that he neglected to draw the inference that partner was marked with a fair amount of strength. Lacking any entries, his heart lead was unlikely to be correct, and he should have tried to hit his partner's suit. He had potential help to offer in spades and diamonds and either suit could have been the right one to lead, but the extra clue that North and South were playing Stayman (which my friend, in his general state of unconsciousness, also failed to note), plus the fact that unbid majors tend to be more promising places to look for tricks than unbid minors, should have decided the issue in favor of the spade lead.

Keeping track of the opponents' Stayman bids can unmask an apparently unbid suit as being one the enemy does in fact hold, and a close decision can sometimes be effectively resolved by taking note of the opponents' failure to use Stayman. However, don't abuse this principle by applying it excessively; make your natural lead when you have one. Holding

♠ 7 4 3   ♡ A 6   ◊ A Q 8 6 4   ♣ J 5 3

lead the six of diamonds if the auction proceeds 1 NT–3 NT whether or not the opponents are playing Stayman. Your diamond strength and high cards provide much more valuable information regarding the most probable method for defeating the contract than does the opponents' failure to seek out a major-suit game.

It is not the purpose of this book to enumerate every possible inference that might be drawn from the opponents' bidding; such a list would be extremely difficult to compile and tiresome to read. Bridge can hardly be fun if it involves endless amounts of memory work. Once you have acquired the habit of listening to the opponents' bidding and asking yourself what their bids are likely to show, you will find that this general strategy will direct you to many winning leads—and that you will have fun drawing your deductions and applying your detective powers. You won't always be right, of course, because the opening leader is working with limited amounts of information, and an unexpected lie of the cards can defeat even the most carefully chosen opening lead. You will, however, win far more often than the majority of players who mechanically follow rules without regard to the specific situation. Perhaps the only time that you may be tempted to regret your eavesdropping on the opponents' bidding conversation is when the information you get is far from clear, as in the following example:

NORTH	SOUTH	YOU (WEST) HOLD
—	1 ♡	♠ J 8 6 ♡ Q 10 6 5 ◇ 8 6 3 ♣ K J 4
2 ♣	2 ◇	
2 ♠	2 NT	
3 NT	Pass	

Horrors! The opponents have bid all four suits, and none of your holdings is strong enough to inspire any confidence as a potential lead. In such situations, make the *safest* lead; here, the eight of diamonds should be selected. If instead you hold

♠ J 8 6   ♡ Q 10 6 5   ◇ Q 6 3   ♣ K J 4

all leads are unattractive (and dangerous), and your best bet is to lead the suit that will need the least help from partner to avoid losing a trick. Lead the five of hearts and hope that partner has (at least) the jack. Had there been an unbid suit, you would prefer to lead it, but unfortunately there is not and you must do your best to find some lead that will not be eagerly seized on by declarer. If you have the spade ten instead of the six, you should lead the jack of spades, as your two touching honors afford some margin of safety.

THE CHOICE OF THE FOURTH-BEST CARD

Having discussed when to lead the fourth-best card from your longest and strongest suit and when to disdain this ancient maxim, it is now time to justify the choice of the fourth-best card. There are two main reasons for selecting this particular card.

First, when you lead fourth-best and follow with a smaller one, partner knows that you originally held five cards in the suit; if you lead the lowest outstanding spot, you cannot hold more than four. For example:

NORTH (dummy)
♠ J 7 6

WEST
♠ 4 led

EAST (you)
♠ A 5 3

SOUTH
?

The four is led, dummy plays small, you win your ace, and South drops the nine. You return the five, South wins the king, and partner drops the deuce. Assuming that he has led from a long suit, his original holding must have been five cards, specifically Q 10 8 4 2, and the suit is ready to run. The information provided by your partner's fourth-best lead will enable you to make a star play if the whole hand is as follows:

NORTH
♠ J 7 6
♡ K 10 9
◇ K Q 7 4
♣ J 10 3

WEST
♠ Q 10 8 4 2
♡ 7 4 3
◇ 8 6
♣ Q 4 2

EAST
♠ A 5 3
♡ 8 6 5 2
◇ 10 3 2
♣ A 8 7

SOUTH
♠ K 9
♡ A Q J
◇ A J 9 5
♣ K 9 6 5

After South opens 1 NT and North raises to 3 NT, the play to the first two tricks proceeds as described above. South now leads a diamond to dummy's king and plays the jack of clubs, hoping to look like a man about to finesse for the queen. Since he also knows from West's plays to the first two tricks that he began with a five-card suit, he reasons that he must go down if West has the club ace and that his only chance is that you (East) have this vital card and will duck the first round of the suit, whereupon he will go right up with the king and quickly run enough tricks in the red suits to make his contract. To give his little swindle the best chance of success, he plays clubs immediately. You know, however, that West has three spades left, so you hop up with your club ace and return a spade to wreck the contract.

NORTH (dummy)
♠ J 7 6

WEST   EAST (you)
♠ 2 led   ♠ A 5

SOUTH
?

In this example, partner's lead of the deuce marks him with no more than a four-card suit, so declarer must also have at least four spades. Therefore, it may well be advisable to win the ace and shift to another suit. Had partner held five spades, you would be more favorably disposed to returning his suit because of the potentially good chance of establishing two length-winners.

The second reason for leading the fourth-best spot is that it allows the partner of the opening leader to put the *rule of eleven* into effect. He simply subtracts the opening leader's card from eleven, and the resulting figure is the number of cards held by the other three players that are higher than the one led. The following example is often cited as a victory for the rule of eleven:

DUMMY
♡ Q 8 3

                   YOU
♡ 7 led   ♡ A 10 4

Subtracting seven, the card led, from eleven leaves four higher cards in the other three hands. You can see all four of them—two in dummy and two in your own hand—so declarer can't have any at all (unless partner's lead is "top of nothing," in which case your play to the first trick makes little difference). If dummy's eight is played, you should put on the ten, for the ace will give declarer an undeserved trick later with the queen, and if dummy's three is played you can even afford to play small. The complete holding:

DUMMY
♡ Q 8 3

PARTNER   YOU
♡ K J 9 7   ♡ A 10 4

DECLARER
♡ 6 5 2

The difficulty with this example is that declarer needs a good peek to play a low card from dummy; his proper play is to go up with the queen in the hope that your partner has led from the ace-king. About all that the rule of eleven can accomplish in this case is to keep you from following an absurd play by declarer with one of your own. A more respectable example is the following:

DUMMY
♠ A 10 7

♠ 5 led   YOU
                                 ♠ Q 9 3

Dummy plays the seven, and your proper play is the nine, not the queen. Subtracting five from eleven leaves six cards higher than the one led distributed between you, declarer, and dummy. Dummy has three and you have two, so declarer can have only one. If it is the six or eight, your nine will win the trick; if it is the jack, you could not have prevented declarer from taking two tricks in the suit no matter what card you played. If, however, declarer has the king, the play of the queen will give him three spade tricks, for he will be able to finesse the ten on the next round. The complete holding:

DUMMY
♠ A 10 7

PARTNER   YOU
♠ J 8 6 5 4   ♠ Q 9 3

DECLARER
♠ K 2

Your play of the nine limits declarer to two spade tricks.

A serious difficulty with the eleven rule is that declarer can get as much or more information from it than do the defenders. For example:

DUMMY
◊ A Q 9 2

WEST   EAST
◊ 6 led   ?

DECLARER
◊ 8 4 3

Assuming that the lead is fourth-best, declarer can simply subtract six from eleven and place five higher cards in the hands of himself, dummy, and his right-hand opponent. Four of these are accounted for—the eight, nine, queen, and ace—so East can have only one. Declarer can ensure three tricks in the suit by playing small from dummy; as it happens, East wins with the ten. West, however, must have the missing king, jack, and seven, so on the next round of the suit dummy's nine is finessed, and later the finesse of the queen is taken. The complete holding:

DUMMY
◊ A Q 9 2

WEST   EAST
◊ K J 7 6   ◊ 10 5

SOUTH
◊ 8 4 3

Rather than give declarer such useful information, many players prefer to make less revealing opening leads. Some modern lead techniques are discussed in the Appendix.

LEADING PARTNER'S SUIT

When partner has bid a suit, fourth-best considerations are usually not a factor. If partner has enough cards in the suit to bid it and declarer has enough to bid notrump, you are unlikely to have as many as four cards in the suit, and the primary question that you will usually face is whether or not to lead partner's suit with a relatively weak holding. The best rule to follow is to lead partner's suit unless you have a very good reason to do otherwise. For example:

(a)	♠ Q 10 8 6	(b)	♠ 7 3 2	(c)	♠ J 9 6 4 3 2
	♡ J 10 3		♡ Q J 10 8 6		♡ 8 5
	◊ 8 7		◊ 5		◊ 7
	♣ K 6 5 4		♣ A 9 8 2		♣ 8 4 3 2

The bidding:

NORTH	EAST	SOUTH	WEST (you)
1 ♣	1 ◊	1 NT	Pass
2 NT	Pass	3 NT	Pass
Pass	Pass		

With hand (a), lead the eight of diamonds. There is no reason to lead a three- or four-card suit when partner has suggested a specific lead.

Lead the queen of hearts on hand (b). You have a fine heart suit, a probable side entry, and poor diamonds.

On hand (c), lead the seven of diamonds. Ordinarily, you would not lead a singleton, but partner has bid the suit and you have no good reason to go against his wishes.

In all of the above hands, your holding in partner's suit was quite poor; with strength in his suit, it is almost always correct to lead it. You should lead low from three to an honor and from any four-card holding, and lead the top from three small cards.

If both you and your partner have bid suits and the enemy arrives at a notrump contract, you should tend to lead partner's suit unless your own is strong. If you are wrong, you can take him to task for bidding such poor suits; but if you lead your own suit and are wrong it is you who will be on the receiving end of the lecture. However, temper your judgment with a knowledge of partner's bidding style. If he tends to overcall on shabby suits, give more thought to leading your own. Some examples:

(a) ♠ A Q 4 3 2   (b) ♠ K Q 10 9 4
     ♡ A 4 3   ♡ A 4 3
     ◇ 10 9 3   ◇ 10 3
     ♣ 7 2   ♣ 7 3 2

The bidding:

NORTH	EAST	SOUTH	WEST (you)
1 ♣	1 ◇	1 ♡	1 ♠
2 ♣	Pass	2 NT	Pass
3 NT	Pass	Pass	Pass

You should lead the ten of diamonds with hand (a); even if the nine of diamonds is changed to a small club, the diamond ten is the proper lead. Had partner not bid, you would lead the three of spades. On (b), however, lead the king of spades.*

---

* Some players treat the lead of the queen as asking partner to unblock the jack on the first trick if he has it, and with this understanding the lead of the queen is preferable. If partner has the jack, you want to know about it in a hurry so that you can keep on playing spades; if declarer has the guarded ace-jack and ducks the first trick, a spade continuation will give him two tricks in the suit.

Of course, if partner supports your suit during the bidding, you have all the more reason to lead it even if it has some flaws.

LEADS AGAINST LOWER-LEVEL NOTRUMP CONTRACTS

In this chapter, 3 NT contracts have been emphasized because many of the principles involved also relate to lower-level notrump contracts, and because defense against notrump partscore contracts is often extremely involved; a full treatment of this topic is beyond the scope of this book. In general, you will not go far wrong in following the ideas discussed in this chapter for 1 and 2 NT contracts as well as notrump games. Note that since the opponents have stopped short of game, they are likely to have fewer than 26 high-card points, a fact which will help you to determine partner's probable strength. Also, it is better to be passive in doubtful situations. The overall strength is more evenly divided, so you are less likely to have to rush to collect the tricks that belong to you, and declarer will probably have to lose the lead more often, giving you a chance to make new attacks with the additional information available from the dummy. You should still be pleased to lead from good five-card and longer suits and solid and nearly solid four-card suits, but you should tend to avoid broken four-card suits unless the bidding or the rest of your hand suggests otherwise. For example:

	NORTH	SOUTH	YOU (WEST) HOLD:
(a)	— Pass	1 NT	♠ Q 10 3 2 ♡ 8 5 3 ◇ K Q 7 ♣ A 6 5
(b)	1 ♡ Pass	1 NT	♠ K J 7 3 ♡ Q J 9 7 ◇ 10 9 3 ♣ A 4
(c)	1 ♣ 1 ♠ Pass	1 ♡ 1 NT	♠ K 6 4 ♡ Q 8 5 ◇ Q 10 8 3 ♣ Q 7 2

(d) —   1 NT   ♠ A J 8 6 3   ♡ K 8 5   ◇ 7 3 2
    2 NT   Pass   ♣ 6 4

On hand (a), anything could be right, and a bad guess is likely to help declarer in his quest for a mere seven tricks. Lead the heart eight and let him do his own work.

You would lead the heart queen in hand (b) even against a 1 NT contract had North not bid the suit because your holding is nearly solid, but on the actual auction you should seek a lead elsewhere. With hearts stopped, you will probably have time to make a switch later if necessary. Play safe and lead the ten of diamonds, noting that South's response shows 6 to 9 points and that dummy is expected to have the better hand.

On hand (c), your middle diamond spots are quite respectable and diamonds are the unbid suit, so lead the three of diamonds.

On hand (d), there is no reason whatsoever to be deterred from the normal lead of the six of spades.

LEADS AFTER A 2 NT OPENING BID

If an opponent opens the bidding with 2 NT and the enemy subsequently plays a notrump contract, go passive in most situations. Your right-hand opponent is marked with such great high-card strength that a lead away from an honor is likely to be fatal. Unless you have a nearly solid suit or a very fine five-card or longer suit with some likely entries, find a worthless tripleton or four-card suit (you are likely to have one in view of the bidding) and let declarer do his own work. Especially if 2 NT is passed out, declarer may never be able to get to dummy and may desperately wish for you to take his finesses for him; even if 2 NT is raised to 3 NT, dummy is likely to be short of entries. If declarer is forced to lead from his hand, potentially winning finesses may turn into tricks for the defense. The 2 NT opening often inspires gloom in the hearts of the defenders, but it may also be a sign of hope in that the opponents' strength is placed in an unwieldy fashion—all in one hand. Take advantage of this fact by making passive leads and not taking any finesses for declarer.

LEADS AFTER A 3 NT OPENING BID

If an opponent bids a "standard" 3 NT opening, showing about 25–27 high-card points, the above warning applies to an even greater extent—go passive and don't take any finesses for declarer. Some players, however, use the 3 NT opening as a gambling bid based on a solid seven- or eight-card minor suit and a high card or two on the side, such as

$$\spadesuit K\,3 \qquad \heartsuit Q\,7 \qquad \diamond 3 \qquad \clubsuit A\,K\,Q\,J\,7\,6\,4\,2$$

The idea is that if a favorable opening lead is made, the gambling 3 NT bidder will be able to run off a great many tricks and perhaps "steal" a game that should not be made. To prevent this dire occurrence, you should lead an ace if you have one. If the opponents ever gain the lead, they will probably be able to cash enough tricks to make their game, so your only chance is to run a suit quickly. Leading an ace gives you a chance to look at dummy and get more information as to what running suit your side may have.

Obviously, it makes quite a bit of difference what kind of 3 NT opening bid your opponents are using, and the wise men who promulgated the laws of bridge decreed that any conventional treatments (such as a gambling 3 NT opening) must be called to the attention of the opponents. Thus, you will always know whether the 3 NT opening bid is standard or the gambling variety.

Review Quiz

In each of the following problems, your right-hand opponent opens 1 NT and is raised to 3 NT by his partner. What card do you lead?

(1)	♠ Q 10 5	♡ K Q 8 5 3	◇ K 8 3	♣ 7 2
(2)	♠ 9 4 3	♡ Q 5 3	◇ 8 6 3	♣ J 7 4 2
(3)	♠ Q J 9 8	♡ K 8 3	◇ J 7 5 4 3	♣ 10
(4)	♠ A Q 6 2	♡ A Q 8 5	◇ 10 9 8 7	♣ 7
(5)	♠ 6 3	♡ A 8 5	◇ Q 10 8 7	♣ Q 7 6 3
(6)	♠ 6 3 2	♡ A Q 7 6 5	◇ Q J 10 4	♣ J
(7)	♠ 8 6 3	♡ Q 5	◇ 8 6 5 4 3 2	♣ K 7
(8)	♠ 7 5 3	♡ A J 10 9 4	◇ 8 6	♣ 5 4 3
(9)	♠ Q 6 3	♡ A J 7	◇ K J 3	♣ 8 7 4 2
(10)	♠ A 7 5	♡ K 6	◇ K Q 7	♣ 8 6 5 3 2
(11)	♠ K 9 8 6 3	♡ 7	◇ Q J 10 6 2	♣ 8 3
(12)	♠ J 8	♡ K 4	◇ 9 7 5 3	♣ 8 6 4 3 2

In the following problems, the auction proceeds as shown. What card do you lead?

(13)

NORTH	EAST	SOUTH	WEST
—	—	1 ◇	1 ♠
2 ♣	Pass	2 NT	Pass
3 NT	Pass	Pass	Pass

You (West) hold:

♠ A Q 8 6 5   ♡ A Q 8 6 5   ◇ 7 2   ♣ 3

(14)

NORTH	EAST	SOUTH	WEST
—	—	1 NT	Pass
2 ♣*	Pass	2 ♠	Pass
3 NT	Pass	Pass	Pass

You (West) hold:

♠ 8 7   ♡ Q J 9 6   ◇ Q 10 8 4   ♣ A 10 3

* Stayman

(15)	NORTH	EAST	SOUTH	WEST
	1 ♣	1 ♦	1 NT	Pass
	2 NT	Pass	3 NT	Pass
	Pass	Pass		

You (West) hold:

♠ J 10 9 8 6   ♡ A K 3   ♦ 2   ♣ 8 4 3 2

(16)	NORTH	EAST	SOUTH	WEST
	—	—	3 NT*	Pass
	Pass	Pass		

You (West) hold:

♠ Q J 10 9 3   ♡ 8 5 3   ♦ A 7 5 4   ♣ 5

(17)	NORTH	EAST	SOUTH	WEST
	—	—	2 NT	Pass
	3 NT	Pass	Pass	Pass

You (West) hold:

♠ Q 9 7 5   ♡ K Q 4 3   ♦ 8 5 3   ♣ A 7

(18)	NORTH	EAST	SOUTH	WEST
	1 ♦	Pass	2 ♣	Pass
	2 ♠	Pass	2 NT	Pass
	3 ♣	Pass	3 ♠	Pass
	3 NT	Pass	Pass	Pass

You (West) hold:

♠ 7   ♡ J 9 4 2   ♦ J 10 6 3   ♣ K J 8 5

* "gambling"

(19)

NORTH	EAST	SOUTH	WEST
—	—	1 NT	Pass
Pass	Pass		

You (West) hold:

♠ Q 10 9 8 6   ♡ A K 3   ◇ 8 5 3   ♣ 7 4

(20)

NORTH	EAST	SOUTH	WEST
—	—	1 ◇	Pass
1 ♠	Pass	1 NT	Pass
2 NT	Pass	3 NT	Pass
Pass	Pass		

You (West) hold:

♠ A 6   ♡ K J 4   ◇ J 10 9 6 5   ♣ A 8 3

(21)

NORTH	EAST	SOUTH	WEST
—	—	1 NT	Pass
Pass	Pass		

You (West) hold:

♠ Q 8 6 4   ♡ 7 3 2   ◇ Q J 6   ♣ K 10 7

(22)

NORTH	EAST	SOUTH	WEST
—	—	2 NT	Pass
Pass	Pass		

You (West) hold:

♠ J 10 9 7   ♡ A 7 3 2   ◇ J 7   ♣ 7 6 3

(23)

NORTH	EAST	SOUTH	WEST
—	1 ♡	1 NT	Pass
2 NT	Pass	3 NT	Pass
Pass	Pass		

You (West) hold:

♠ J 10 7 4 3   ♥ 8 2   ◊ Q J 6   ♣ 10 5 2

(24)	NORTH	EAST	SOUTH	WEST
	1 ◊	Pass	1 NT	Pass
	2 NT	Pass	3 NT	Pass
	Pass	Pass		

You (West) hold:

♠ 10 9 8   ♥ J 9 8   ◊ A 9 8 7   ♣ 10 9 8

(25)	NORTH	EAST	SOUTH	WEST
	1 ♣	1 ♠	2 ♣	Pass
	2 ♥	Pass	2 NT	Pass
	3 NT	Pass	Pass	Pass

You (West) hold:

♠ Q 6 3   ♥ 8 5 2   ◊ Q J 10 9   ♣ 8 4 3

Solutions

(1)   *Five of hearts*   You have a good suit to establish and several potential entries.

(2)   *Three of hearts*   With a weak hand, you should try and hit partner's suit. An unbid major is a better bet than an unbid minor, and you should prefer the major in which you can offer some help.

(3)   *Queen of spades*   Prefer the nearly solid four-card suit to the weak five-card suit. If the spades were K J 9 8, a diamond lead would be correct.

(4)   *Ten of diamonds*   Avoid the lead from A Q x x.

(5)   *Seven of diamonds*   Prefer the stronger suit.

(6)   *Six of hearts*   One lead may establish the suit. A lead from a *strong* five-card suit is likely to be very

effective and should be preferred to a four-card sequence.

(7) *Eight of spades* It is better to try and hit partner's suit than to lead the pitiful diamond suit with so few entries, and a three-card major is likely to be a better bet than a doubleton.

(8) *Jack of hearts* Play to establish your good suit, and remember to lead the top of an interior sequence.

(9) *Eight of clubs* The other suits are too unattractive to lead from, and your hand is too strong to warrant an all-out attempt to hit partner's suit (he can't have much strength). The highest card is chosen to tell partner that if he gains the lead, a shift to a new suit would be welcomed.

(10) *Three of clubs* With five cards in the suit, you wish to encourage partner to return a club if he gains the lead. You plan to use your side-suit high cards as entries to establish clubs.

(11) *Queen of diamonds* Since your suits are of equal length, prefer the one that is more solid.

(12) *King of hearts* An unusual but justified attempt to hit partner's suit in view of the poor hand (placing partner with some strength) and lack of entries to develop your own weak suits. You select the major suit in which you can offer the most help. As it happens, partner has ♡ A 10 7 5 3 and a side ace, the enemy's hearts divide 3-3, and the heart lead (establishing the suit before partner's side ace is dislodged) is the only play to defeat the contract.

(13) *Six of hearts* South is prepared for your spade length and strength; the unannounced heart suit may be an unpleasant surprise.

(14) *Four of diamonds* North is marked with a four-card heart suit because of his Stayman bid and subsequent disinterest in spades, so the more solid heart suit (which would ordinarily be preferred) should be rejected.

(15) *Jack of spades* With two probable side entries, a solid suit, and a singleton in partner's suit, you have good reason to prefer the lead of your own suit.

(16)   *Ace of diamonds*   Lead an ace against a "gambling" 3 NT bid if you have one. As the cards lie, South can take seven club tricks and the ace-king of spades; your side can run five diamond tricks. Were spades your suit, there would still be time to switch after the ace lead.

(17)   *Eight of diamonds*   Go passive against a 2 NT opening bid.

(18)   *Two of hearts*   The opponents seem to be somewhat unhappy about the unbid suit, and no other lead is attractive.

(19)   *Ten of spades*   With a good five-card suit, make your normal lead even against a 1 NT contract.

(20)   *Six of diamonds*   With most of the outstanding high cards, play to set up your own suit. You would lead the jack had the suit not been bid on your right.

(21)   *Seven of hearts*   When in doubt, go passive against low-level notrump contracts.

(22)   *Jack of spades*   Sometimes the safest lead is also the most constructive. The spade is least likely to help declarer, and may (as a fringe benefit) set up a trick or two for your side.

(23)   *Eight of hearts*   You have no reason to disregard partner's recommendation.

(24)   *Ten of clubs*   With a weak hand, try and hit partner's suit. While you would usually prefer to lead an unbid major, partner's failure to overcall in either hearts or spades at the one-level suggests that he is not "loaded" in either of these suits. A two-level overcall, however, requires considerable strength and he might have had to pass even with a fairly good club holding.

(25)   *Three of spades*   With considerable help in partner's suit, the diamond sequence should present no temptation. If declarer is hoping for two spade stoppers with a holding such as K J 4, he will be in for a rude awakening when partner wins the opening lead with the ace and returns a low spade to your queen.

5

Leads Against Suit Contracts

♠ ♡ ◇ ♣

To a declarer, few things in life are worse than when you run an established suit against him. He is forced to sit by in utter frustration while you take tricks by relentlessly leading out cards to which neither he nor dummy can follow suit. Often he must discard winners on your good tricks, adding insult and increasing the amount of injury.

To prevent this catastrophe, the declaring side will often choose to name a suit as trumps. This clever ploy will help to foil you in your attempt to establish winners and defeat the contract, for declarer will be able to call a halt to your fun by inserting a trump whenever he is unable to follow suit. In addition to stopping the run of length-winners, ruffing may also enable declarer to deprive the defenders' high cards of their power and get rid of some of his losing small cards. Unfortunately, you are less likely to be able to reciprocate by ruffing declarer's winners, for he is not at all democratic about the selection of a trump suit and seeks out one in which his side holds a substantially greater number of cards. Unless all trumps should happen to be played at some point (in which case you are in effect playing at notrump, length-winners will come into their own, and your high cards will be safe from the ruffing menace), declarer will have an advantage. He will be able to develop some length-winners by first extracting your trumps so that you cannot ruff, while your length-winners (and possibly some strength-winners as well) will fall victim to the ample supply of trumps at his command. This is indeed a gloomy picture, but all is far from lost, for you still retain the right to make the first play and a good opening lead can give your side an important advantage.

For example:

```
                    NORTH
                    ♠ A 10 5 4
                    ♡ 7
                    ◊ 10 5 4 3
                    ♣ A 10 9 2

        WEST                        EAST
        ♠ 8 2                       ♠ J 9 7
        ♡ A 10 6 4 3 2              ♡ J 9 8
        ◊ 9 7                       ◊ A 8 6 2
        ♣ K Q J                     ♣ 8 7 4

                    SOUTH
                    ♠ K Q 6 3
                    ♡ K Q 5
                    ◊ K Q J
                    ♣ 6 5 3
```

The bidding:

SOUTH	WEST	NORTH	EAST
1 NT	2 ♡	3 ♡	Pass
3 ♠	Pass	4 ♠	Pass
Pass	Pass		

North and South would not have fared very well had they tried for game in notrump. West, seeking to build length-winners, would lead the heart four. South would win the first trick, but when East gained the lead with the ace of diamonds he would return a heart and West would run his suit to defeat the contract two tricks. An opening club lead, on the other hand, would hold the defense to four tricks—much to East's displeasure.

To eliminate the threat of length-winners, North and South properly sought out the spade game. North was unable to make a Stayman 2 ♣ response because of West's overcall, so he cleverly improvised by cue-bidding 3 ♡, and South had no trouble deciding what to do. This time, a heart lead would be fatal for the defense. If West should cash the ace, declarer would gratefully pitch two low clubs from dummy on his king and queen and lose only one club, one diamond, and one heart. If West leads a low heart, declarer will take his heart king and ruff the queen and the five, thus losing only two clubs and a diamond. If, however, West leads a club, declarer is rendered helpless and East is immensely pleased, for when East gains the lead with the diamond ace the defenders will quickly cash two club winners and the heart ace to defeat the contract before declarer can obtain any discards. How does West decide on clubs? By realizing that against a suit contract, quick winners which will not fall victim to declarer's ruffs must be developed. (As we will see later, an exception occurs when you think that you can exhaust declarer's trumps and leave him no weapon with which to combat your length-winners.) Fortunately, developing quick tricks is a more feasible plan against a suit (rather than a notrump) declaration, for distribution points will comprise part of declarer's total count and more high-card strength is likely to be at the disposal of the defenders. Let's look at some of the procedures available to you for bringing about declarer's downfall with an effective opening lead.

CONCENTRATIONS OF STRENGTH

A suit in which you hold a solid or nearly solid sequence is often a good place to begin the attack against declarer's contract, provided of course that there are no strong indications to the contrary from the bidding. The lead from holdings such as

$$A K J 5, \quad K Q J 7 3, \quad Q J 10, \quad \text{or } J 10 9 6$$

has the potential advantage of building up tricks quickly for your side without giving away any tricks that declarer could not otherwise get by himself. Similarly, nearly solid sequences such as

$$K Q 10 4, \quad Q J 9 7, \quad \text{and } J 10 8 7$$

are also theoretically attractive choices, though involving somewhat more risk than the solid sequences. Since the fates have conspired to deal the opponents the majority of the outstanding strength, partner's spirit may be willing but his cards woefully weak. Consequently, when the bidding fails to indicate the probable location of assistance in partner's hand, it is good sense to lead a suit which does not require much help. Even if no aid is forthcoming from partner, the defense may still be on the right track. If, on the other hand, you lead from a weaker holding, you are incurring more risk. Compare the following examples:

NORTH

♠ A 6 3

WEST   EAST

♠ K Q 4 2   ♠ 9 8 7

SOUTH

♠ J 10 5

West's lead of the king gives declarer two spade tricks. If West refuses to lead spades and covers any honor South may lead, declarer will get only one trick in spades.

NORTH

♠ A 6 3

WEST   EAST

♠ K Q 10 2   ♠ 9 8 7

SOUTH

♠ J 5 4

The lead of the king in this example sets up two spade tricks for the defense if North's ace is played, and gives the defense one trick in the bag and declarer no assistance if North plays low. The lead still entails some danger, however, as it would cost a trick if the positions of the spade ace and jack were reversed.

NORTH
♠ A 6 3

WEST   EAST
♠ K Q J 10   ♠ 9 8 7

SOUTH
♠ 5 4 2

This time, West's spade lead establishes two potential winners for the defense and cannot cost a trick no matter how the North-South cards are arranged.

In each case, West is unfortunate to find no assistance forthcoming from his partner, but can stand this adversity better when his suit is strong.

The holding of A Q J is risky to lead from because if declarer has the king, he will get a trick he does not deserve. However, the advantage of leading from this holding when dummy is marked with a very strong hand (perhaps by an opening 1 NT bid) and is likely to hold the king is often overlooked. In this instance, the lead of the ace followed by the queen may establish the jack as a winner without costing anything. With no clues from the bidding or other indication to the contrary, however, you will usually do better to avoid this lead.

Leads from non-sequence strength may or may not be desirable. More risk is involved than in the case of even a weak sequence such as K Q 4 2. For example, a lead from K J 7 or K 8 6 3 is likely to lose a trick, or at best waste time, without gaining anything in return unless partner holds specifically the ace or queen. Leads from broken suits headed by the jack, such as J 8 7 4, are also poor in theory. One well-known expert has gone so far as to forbid any of his partners ever to lead from a jack; what they are supposed to do with hands such as

♠ J 8 6 5   ♡ J 7 3   ◇ J 8 6 4   ♣ J 7

remains a mystery (perhaps toss their cards out the window, or leave the room on a pretext and never return). The theoretical disadvantage of a lead, however, is often outweighed in practice by the clues and inferences that are available to you. For example, partner may bid the suit, the suit may be conspicuously unbid by the opponents, or the opponents' bidding may suggest that they have plenty of winners available for discards and that you will have to get busy and take tricks in the suit in a hurry. Similarly, leads from queens are commonly regarded as theoretically better than leads from the other honors, but this applies only to situations where the bidding offers little or no information to the opening leader.

PASSIVE LEADS

When you are faced with a collection of unpleasant suits to lead from and the bidding is not informative, your main goal will usually be to avoid giving any free gifts to declarer. For example:

♠ K 3   ♡ A Q 8 2   ◊ 8 6 3   ♣ A 10 4 2

The bidding:

OPPONENT	YOU	OPPONENT	PARTNER
1 ♠	Double	2 ♠	Pass
Pass	Pass		

There does not appear to be any hurry to establish winners, so the risk of giving away a trick makes the lead from any of the honor holdings unattractive. Lead the diamond eight. The club ace may seem safe, but it should be reserved to capture the enemy's honor cards; if it is led it will collect only low spots. The whole situation might be:

DUMMY
♣ Q 8 5

YOU   PARTNER
♣ A 10 4 2   ♣ J 9 7

DECLARER
♣ K 6 3

Leading a club gives declarer two tricks in the suit where nature intended him to have only one. At times you will hold unconnected honors in all four suits, and this embarrassment of riches will force you to make an aggressive lead. In such cases, the least risky may be the best:

♠ A J 7   ♡ Q 8 5   ◇ Q 10 4 2   ♣ K 9 6

The bidding:

OPPONENT	YOU	OPPONENT	PARTNER
1 ♡	Pass	3 ♡	Pass
4 ♡	Pass	Pass	Pass

The diamond deuce is safest and also may help your side establish tricks if partner has as little as the jack by way of assistance.

TRICK ESTABLISHMENT AND SUIT LENGTH

Given a choice between two unbid suits of approximately equal strength, should you prefer to lead from the longer or from one that is moderately short? For example:

♠ 9 8 6   ♡ 8 7   ◇ Q 8 6 5 4   ♣ Q 7 5

The opponents are playing a heart contract and have bid spades; both minor suits are unbid. In this situation, a diamond lead (the longer unbid suit) is *safer,* but is *less likely to establish several tricks* for your side. A club lead (the shorter unbid suit), on the other hand, is *more dangerous,* but is *more likely to establish several tricks* for your side. Even if your long-suit lead hits partner's strength, declarer or dummy is likely to be able to ruff in and severely limit the number of tricks you can take. (Your length, however, represents protection against giving the enemy undeserved tricks, because their honor cards are likely to be poorly protected and because they are less likely to want to set up length-winners in this suit.) Conversely, declarer and dummy each probably have a few cards in your shorter suit, so if you hit partner's strength you will be able to take a few tricks before a pestiferous trump enters the scene. When partner does not have strength in the suit, however, you're playing into declarer's strength *and* length, a situation which is likely to prove disastrous.

In summary, if you have reason to think that you must hurry to take tricks (perhaps because dummy has promised a strong and long suit which may be established for discards), lead your shorter suit. If the bidding is uninformative and you want to reduce the chances of giving away anything on the opening lead, prefer your long suit.

CLUES FROM THE BIDDING

When the opponents bid nothing but their trump suit, you obtain relatively little information to help you in your choice of opening lead. Often, however, the enemy will not decide on a trump suit until some discussion has taken place, allowing you to obtain useful facts by listening in. Here are some of the deductions you can make:

Are you in trouble? For instance, does the dummy possess a long suit on which declarer, given time, can discard his losers? Consider the following deal, taken from the April 1959 *Bridge World:*

WEST (you)	NORTH	EAST	SOUTH
1 ♠	Double	2 ♠	3 ◇
4 ♠	5 ◇	Pass	Pass
Double	Pass	Pass	Pass

You hold:

♠ Q J 10 7 5　　♡ A K J　　◇ 3　　♣ A Q J 6

What is your lead?

A takeout double of one major suit usually promises strength in the other, so North should be fairly well off in hearts. Therefore, the danger exists that South may have a singleton heart and set up North's suit by ruffing out your high-card winners. If so, you had better set up some club winners in a hurry; even one round of any other suit may be too many. Since North is marked with most of the missing high-card strength, he probably has the club king, and the lead of the club ace is unlikely to lose and may well gain. The complete deal may be:

NORTH
♠ A
♡ Q 10 7 6 4
◇ K Q 7 2
♣ K 8 5

WEST
♠ Q J 10 7 5
♡ A K J
◇ 3
♣ A Q J 6

EAST
♠ K 9 6 4 2
♡ 8 5 3 2
◇ 8 4
♣ 9 3

SOUTH
♠ 8 3
♡ 9
◇ A J 10 9 6 5
♣ 10 7 4 2

A club lead establishes two quick winners in that suit for the defense, and the ace of hearts provides the setting trick. You would ordinarily be happy to lead from Q J 10 in a suit bid by you and supported by partner, or from A K J, but here both leads cost the contract. With a spade lead, for example, dummy wins and plays a heart; West wins and plays the ace and queen of clubs. Dummy wins the club king, a heart is ruffed in the South hand, and declarer enters dummy with a high diamond to ruff out West's last high heart. Dummy is entered with the remaining high diamond, exhausting the defenders' trumps, South's two low clubs are discarded on the queen and ten of hearts, and declarer easily takes the rest of the tricks to make his doubled contract. Leading the king of hearts produces the same unfortunate result.

A second unhappy situation occurs when you have reason to believe that the cards are lying well for declarer. For example, suppose you hold

♠ K J 8   ♡ Q 3 2   ♢ 7 3 2   ♣ K J 7 5

(a)	OPPONENT	YOU	OPPONENT	PARTNER
	—	—	1 ♠	Pass
	2 ♡	Pass	2 ♠	Pass
	3 ♢	Pass	3 ♡	Pass
	4 ♡	Pass	Pass	Pass

(b)	OPPONENT	YOU	OPPONENT	PARTNER
	1 ♡	Pass	2 ♡	Pass
	2 ♠	Pass	3 ♡	Pass
	4 ♡	Pass	Pass	Pass

In example (a), you can deduce from your hand and the bidding that things are likely to go depressingly well for declarer. Your spade honors are in front of the dummy's, so any spade finesses are likely to work, and your lack of spade length will make it relatively easy for declarer to ruff out your king. To add to the general gloom, any diamond honors that your side holds are in front of declarer's bid suit and are therefore subject to some devastating finesses. As a result, you had better try to build up some tricks in a hurry; the unbid club suit offers the best chance and is worth the risk of a possible gift to declarer. Lead the five of clubs.

On hand (b), however, you have no reason to rush; and declarer, who has driven the hand to game even though his partner has promised only 6 or 7 points, is clearly "loaded" and likely to hold some or all of the missing club honors. Therefore, go passive and lead the diamond seven.

A third troublesome instance is when the opponents' bidding is full of zip and they rush into game with no second thoughts. In this case, you should figure them for values over and above those needed for game and thus look for tricks you can claim in a hurry. If, however, the opponents get to game only after a grim struggle, any gift on the opening lead may be just enough to allow them to bring home the contracts, so greater caution is preferable. Some sample auctions:

(a) | SOUTH | NORTH |
     |-------|-------|
     | 1 ♠ | 2 ◊ |
     | 2 ♠ | 4 ♠ |
     | Pass | |

The opponents have had no problem reaching game; South has a minimum or near minimum hand, but North is not in the least dismayed. Some aggressiveness is therefore warranted; holding

♠ K 8 3   ♡ Q 7 3   ◊ 6 5 3   ♣ J 7 4 2

lead the three of hearts.

(b) | SOUTH | NORTH |
     |-------|-------|
     | 1 ♠ | 2 ♠ |
     | 3 ♠ | 4 ♠ |
     | Pass | |

Here, the opponents have struggled slowly up to 4 ♠ and should not have much left over. Caution is indicated, and your best bet, with the same hand, is the passive diamond six lead.

Strong and weak spots: Suppose you are West and hold

♠ Q J 9 8   ♡ J 8 6   ◊ K 10 3   ♣ 6 4 2

What do you lead against each of the following auctions?

(a) | SOUTH | WEST | NORTH | EAST |
     |-------|------|-------|------|
     | 1 ♡ | Pass | 3 ♡ | Pass |
     | 4 ♡ | Pass | Pass | Pass |

(b) | SOUTH | WEST | NORTH | EAST |
     |-------|------|-------|------|
     | — | — | 1 ♠ | Pass |
     | 2 ♡ | Pass | 4 ♡ | Pass |
     | Pass | Pass | | |

(c)	SOUTH	WEST	NORTH	EAST
	—	—	1 ♠	Pass
	2 ♣	Pass	3 ♣	Pass
	3 ♡	Pass	4 ♣	Pass
	5 ♣	Pass	Pass	Pass

In example (a), you have little information to go on and should lead the queen of spades, choosing to begin the attack with your nearly solid sequence.

Given auction (b), a spade lead is unattractive, for dummy is marked with length in spades and a good hand and declarer may well want to develop spades himself. The diamond holding is also unappealing to lead from, so the best choice is the club six.

In auction (c), the opponents have opted for the eleven-trick club game rather than a potentially easier nine-trick no-trump game, and the bidding suggests that alarm over the diamond situation may be the explanation for this seemingly strange behavior. Lead the three of diamonds.

The bidding may also suggest ways in which you can change what the opponents believe to be a strong spot into a cause for grave concern. For example, suppose you hold

♠ A 7   ♡ 9 4 3   ◇ J 6 5 4 2   ♣ A 10 5

and the bidding proceeds as follows:

OPPONENT	YOU	OPPONENT	PARTNER
1 ♠	Pass	2 ◇	Pass
3 ◇	Pass	3 ♠	Pass
4 ♠	Pass	Pass	Pass

Your left-hand opponent has shown at least four diamonds, and possibly more, by his 2 ◇ response; your right-hand opponent has promised at least three-card support by raising to 3 ◇. Therefore, your partner cannot have more than a singleton and may very well be void. Lead the deuce of diamonds. (When entries for ruffs are involved, the lead of a low spot asks partner to return the lower-ranking of the two side suits when he gains the lead—here, clubs rather than hearts.) If partner follows suit, you can still give him a ruff when you win your ace of trumps.

Sometimes your partner will help resolve your opening lead problems by mentioning a suit of his own. For example:

(a)		(b)		(c)	
♠ K 3		♠ J 6 5		♠ K 7 3	
♡ Q 7 4		♡ K 5		♡ 7 6 4	
◊ 10 9 8 5		◊ 10 9 8 5		◊ 10 9 8 5 4 2	
♣ 8 6 5 2		♣ 8 6 5 2		♣ 6	

The bidding:

PARTNER	OPPONENT	YOU	OPPONENT
1 ♡	1 ♠	Pass	3 ♠
Pass	4 ♠	Pass	Pass
Pass			

With hand (a), lead the four of hearts. Leading the queen would give declarer a second heart trick with K J 2.

On hand (b), the heart king is the most attractive choice, as you may be able to get a subsequent ruff or overruff and are unlikely to lose a trick on the lead in view of partner's promise of heart strength.

Holding hand (c), however, lead the club six. Partner is marked with strength because of his opening bid, and you should hope that either he will win the first club and give you a ruff or that you will later gain the lead with the spade king, lead to one of his high cards, and get a ruff at that point.

When leading partner's suit, it is usually correct to lead low from four or more and from three to an honor, and top from a doubleton or three small. (But don't underlead the ace.) Sharp detective work, however, will often point the way to an important exception:

PARTNER	OPPONENT	YOU	OPPONENT
1 ♡	1 ♠	Pass	2 NT
Pass	4 ♠	Pass	Pass
Pass			

You hold:

♠ 5 2   ♥ Q 6 2   ♦ 8 6 3 2   ♣ 9 8 6 4

Dummy's 2 NT bid marks him with some high-card strength in hearts, and your barren collection of cards indicates that never again will you have the privilege of leading (on this deal, anyway). Since it may be necessary to lead twice through dummy's heart strength, lead the *queen* of hearts. The complete deal:

NORTH
♠ K 8
♥ K 9 8
♦ Q J 10 5
♣ A Q J 3

WEST
♠ 5 2
♥ Q 6 2
♦ 8 6 3 2
♣ 9 8 6 4

EAST
♠ Q 7
♥ A J 10 3
♦ A K 9 4
♣ 7 5 2

SOUTH
♠ A J 10 9 6 4 3
♥ 7 5 4
♦ 7
♣ K 10

South has made a bad decision at his final turn to bid; 3 NT played by North cannot be defeated. Admittedly, the seven-card suit is hard to resist. Against the ordinary lead of the heart deuce, however, South's gaffe will not matter, for he will simply insert dummy's eight. East can win with the ten, but can do no better than cash his red aces to hold the contract to four. The inspired lead of the heart queen, however, exacts the full penalty for South's bidding error. It does South no good to play low from dummy when the heart queen is led, for West retains the lead and plays another heart, and the defenders take three heart tricks and a diamond trick before South can get the clubs into action for discards.

In the above deal, the key to the unusual lead of the unsupported honor card in partner's suit was the 2 NT bid, which marked the missing heart strength in dummy. Without this clue, the proper lead would be the heart deuce.

Another situation favoring this unusual lead occurs when your side is marked with all the strength in your partner's suit, and you wish to retain the lead for a possible shift through dummy:

```
                        NORTH
                        ♠ 8 3
                        ♡ K 10 6 4
                        ◇ K 8 4
                        ♣ A Q 10 3
        WEST                            EAST
        ♠ K 7 6 4 2                     ♠ A Q 10 9 5
        ♡ 7 3                           ♡ 9
        ◇ J 6 2                         ◇ A Q 10 3
        ♣ J 6 2                         ♣ 8 5 4
                        SOUTH
                        ♠ J
                        ♡ A Q J 8 5 2
                        ◇ 9 7 5
                        ♣ K 9 7
```

The bidding:

EAST	SOUTH	WEST	NORTH
1 ♠	2 ♡	2 ♠	4 ♡
Pass	Pass	Pass	

If West makes the normal lead of his fourth-best spade, the defenders will soon be complaining about their bad luck, for the 3-3 club split allows declarer to park a losing diamond on dummy's long clubs and fulfill his contract. West's length and strength in East's bid suit makes it extremely unlikely that the king lead will cost, and he has no holding in a side suit that will profit by a lead from partner. Therefore, he should lead his spade honor so he can retain the precious right to play first to the next trick. As it happens, East drops the spade queen at trick one. Since signaling with queens is a startling form of behavior. East must have something special in mind—namely a switch to the higher-ranking side suit, diamonds. West again shows his keen perception of entry considerations by shifting to the *jack* of diamonds at the second trick, and the defense need no longer worry about luck, for they collect three fast diamond tricks and defeat the contract. Needless to say, a low diamond lead at trick two will ruin all the good work accomplished by the stellar opening lead of the spade king, for South will simply play small from dummy and East will be stuck with the lead one trick too soon.

Note that with probable side entries, the lead of an unsupported honor in partner's suit from holdings of three or more cards is unlikely to be necessary, for you will have more chances to lead later on.

TRUMP LEADS

A trump lead should not be made just because you are "in doubt." Rather, it is designed to accomplish a specific purpose. For instance, a good time to lead trump is when the auction suggests that declarer plans on using ruffs to make his contract, and it appears unlikely that the defenders can score any overruffs. Some typical examples of this are:

(a)	SOUTH	NORTH
	1 ◇	1 NT
	2 ♣	Pass

North refuses to return to diamonds in spite of the fact that a player's first-bid suit is usually longer than his second. Apparently, North holds more clubs than diamonds, and South may well plan to ruff diamonds in dummy.

(b)   SOUTH   NORTH
             1 ♡   3 ♡
             3 NT   4 ♡
             Pass

In this example, South opts for a notrump contract but North refuses to accept the idea. Undoubtedly, North sees some virtue in being able to ruff.

(c)   SOUTH   NORTH
             1 ♠   1 NT
             2 ◇   2 ♠
             Pass

Here, North prefers spades to diamonds, yet his spades were not good enough to raise directly. It is reasonable to infer that he is short in both suits and is simply returning to South's longer suit.

In all of the above examples, a trump lead (and continuation when the defense regains the lead) may prevent declarer from making use of his trumps for ruffing purposes. However, *don't* lead a trump if you're very long in declarer's side suit, for partner can probably overruff dummy; and *don't* lead a trump from a holding where it is likely to cost a trick. For example, suppose the auction proceeds as in (c) above and you hold each of the following hands:

(a)   ♠ 7 5 3   (b)   ♠ 5 3   (c)   ♠ K 3
      ♡ 9 7 2   ♡ 9 7 2   ♡ 9 7 2
      ◇ A J 10 2   ◇ A J 8 6 2   ◇ A J 10 2
      ♣ K Q J   ♣ Q J 9   ♣ Q J 9 8

Against South's 2 ♠ contract, the five of spades is an ideal lead with hand (a). Your diamond holding is strong, so that you will find it most painful for declarer to ruff his low cards in that suit in dummy, but not so long as to suggest that partner can profitably overruff. The complete deal might be:

NORTH
♠ J 6
♡ Q 6 5 4 3
◊ 8 3
♣ A 8 5 4

WEST
♠ 7 5 3
♡ 9 7 2
◊ A J 10 2
♣ K Q J

EAST
♠ Q 10 9
♡ K J 10
◊ 9 6 4
♣ 10 9 7 2

SOUTH
♠ A K 8 4 2
♡ A 8
◊ K Q 7 5
♣ 6 3

You lead a spade; South wins, crosses to the club ace, and leads a diamond to his king. You win and lead another trump, and South must lose one trick in spades, one in hearts, one in clubs, and three in diamonds for down one. Any other lead is more to declarer's liking; a club, for example, allows him to play diamonds before any trumps have been drawn. You win your ace and may shift to trumps, but it is too late; declarer scores the critical diamond ruff in dummy and makes his part-score contract.

With hand (b), lead the club queen. Your diamond length and trump shortage suggest that partner is drooling at the thought of overruffing dummy; don't spoil his fun.

Holding hand (c), you would like to lead a trump, but the lead from K 3 is all too likely to cost a trick. Lead the queen of clubs and hope that partner can play trumps through declarer before it is too late.

Another good time to consider leading trump is when the bidding yields no clues to the weak points in the opponent's armament and your side suits are basically unattractive to lead from. Holding

♠ K J 7   ♡ 6 4   ◊ A Q 8 5   ♣ J 7 3 2

against the auction 1 ♡–3 ♡–4 ♡, lead the heart four, not so much to stop ruffs as to avoid giving away anything in the other suits.

You should also lead trump when a low-level takeout double is passed. The pass to a one-level takeout double is a *command* to lead a trump; partner promises that his trumps are strong enough to draw trumps and that your objective should be to prevent the opponents from gaining ruffing tricks. A sample hand:

```
                    NORTH
                    ♠ 8 7 4 3 2
                    ♡ 7 6 3
                    ◇ K 2
                    ♣ 7 4 3
    WEST                          EAST
    ♠ A K 10 6                    ♠ Q J 5
    ♡ 2                           ♡ K Q J 10 9
    ◇ Q J 10 8                    ◇ 9 5 3
    ♣ K Q 8 5                     ♣ 6 2
                    SOUTH
                    ♠ 9
                    ♡ A 8 5 4
                    ◇ A 7 6 4
                    ♣ A J 10 9
```

The bidding (North-South vulnerable):

SOUTH	WEST	NORTH	EAST
1 ♡	Double	Pass	Pass
Pass			

West has holdings of various attractiveness in the side suits, but he has no choice; partner's pass requires that he lead his trump. The heart lead beats the hand two tricks, as declarer cannot take more than his four top winners and one diamond ruff in dummy before East gains the lead and draws trumps. If West leads anything else, South makes his doubled contract. Suppose a diamond is led; South wins the ace and plays a spade. The defenders win and switch to trumps. South wins the heart ace, plays a diamond to dummy's king, ruffs a spade, ruffs a diamond, ruffs another spade, and cashes the club ace for his seventh trick. With this ghastly result in view, East is likely to remark that had he known West would defend that badly, he would have preferred the notrump game that was there for the taking.

Similarly, the following auction also strongly suggests a trump lead:

SOUTH	WEST	NORTH	EAST
1 ♣	1 ◇	2 ♣	Pass
Pass	Double	Pass	Pass
Pass			

West's double is for takeout; when East converts it to penalties by passing, he indicates that he is well off in the trump suit and that the probable winning strategy for the defenders is to draw trumps and keep the enemy from making tricks by ruffing.

Another situation in which you should consider a trump lead is when a one-level contract is passed out and you are short in trumps. Modern technique favors refusing to allow the opponents to play a one-level contract whenever feasible, because such partscores are difficult to defeat and can add up to games if a few are made in a row. Therefore, the player in fourth seat will usually chime in with a takeout double or overcall to fight for the contract and push the opponents up a notch or two. Thus, when partner quietly passes a one-level bid, the implication is that he likes the contract, which in turn suggests that he is well off in trumps and would welcome the lead to cut down the enemy's ruffing power. If you are long and strong in trumps or have a good hand, however, he is probably just plain broke, so make your natural lead.

When you are likely to have the balance of high-card strength and the opponents' most likely source of tricks is ruffing, including the possibility of a complete crossruff, think very seriously about leading a trump. The most significant clues that this situation exists occur when the opponents take a sacrifice against a contract you expect to make on power, or when they dare to enter the auction after your side has opened the bidding with 1 NT. If, for example, you and your partner bid to 4 ♡, confidently expecting to make it by virtue of considerable high-card strength, the opponents intrude by sacrificing at 5 ◇, and you have good holdings in all side (non-trump) suits, lead a trump. You will have time to collect your side-suit winners and may well increase the penalty by cutting down the enemy's ruffing potential. Of course, if you have any reason to fear discards, abandon the trump lead and go after your own winners.

Sometimes warning signals will flash, indicating that a trump lead is likely to be ineffective. Some occasions when the trump lead should be avoided are:

(1) When you fear that declarer will, if given sufficient time, take discards on a side suit. You cannot afford to waste time with a trump lead when this occurs, but must set up your own winning tricks with the utmost speed.

(2) When your trump holding is precarious, and leading from it is likely to cost a trick.

(3) When you have a singleton trump. This is rarely a good lead because you cannot play another trump when you next gain the lead, and because different tactics are desirable if (as would seem to be the case) declarer is running into a bad trump split.

(4) When you have four or more trumps. When declarer receives a disastrous trump break, there are better ways of bringing about his ruination, as we will see in the next section.

THE FORCING GAME

Most of the time, declarer will possess enough trumps to guard against running out, and it will often seem to the anguished defenders as though he had enough for the next five deals. If, however, you have four or more trumps (or a void or singleton, indicating that partner may have considerable length), it may be possible to cause declarer to lose control of the hand by forcing him to ruff until your trumps outnumber his. Here's a typical example of the forcing game in action:

```
                        NORTH
                        ♠ 7 3 2
                        ♡ 10 9 5
                        ◇ 9 6 3 2
                        ♣ A K Q

        WEST                            EAST
        ♠ 9 8 6 5                       ♠ 4
        ♡ 8                             ♡ A 6 4 3 2
        ◇ A K Q J 8                     ◇ 7 5 4
        ♣ 10 9 7                        ♣ 5 4 3 2

                        SOUTH
                        ♠ A K Q J 10
                        ♡ K Q J 7
                        ◇ 10
                        ♣ J 8 6
```

South plays 4 ♠ and appears to have eleven top tricks—five spades, three hearts, and three clubs. An inexperienced West will hold him to ten tricks by leading the singleton heart to East's ace and ruffing the heart return. Unfortunately, declarer laughs last, for he scores up his game. A West player versed in the forcing game leads and continues diamonds. South ruffs (else a heart shift beats the contract immediately), draws two rounds of trumps, winces at the bad split and plays hearts. He cannot draw all the trumps, or his ability to interrupt the run of diamonds will disappear, and East will win the heart ace and return a diamond for West to cash three more winners. East takes his ace and plays another diamond, correctly refusing the temptation to give West a heart ruff. The best that declarer can do now is hold his losses to down one by discarding on the next two rounds of diamonds, ruffing the fifth round in dummy and cashing the three top clubs; in practice he is likely to ruff East's diamond return in a burst of irritation and go down two.

The forcing game can wreck apparently impregnable contracts, and all that is necessary is to keep in mind the general strategy: when holding length in trumps (at least four), do *not* seek ruffs of your own but rather make declarer ruff if at all possible. (Don't make *dummy* ruff; shortening the short trump hand won't bother declarer in the slightest, as the trumps in his hand will still outnumber yours.) Another example:

```
                      NORTH
                      ♠ K Q
                      ♡ J 8 7
                      ◇ 7 5 4 2
                      ♣ A J 8 6
      WEST                              EAST
      ♠ 8 6 3                           ♠ 10 9 7 5 4 2
      ♡ A K Q 2                         ♡ 3
      ◇ Q 10 8 6 3                      ◇ J 9
      ♣ 7                               ♣ 9 5 4 2
                      SOUTH
                      ♠ A J
                      ♡ 10 9 6 5 4
                      ◇ A K
                      ♣ K Q 10 3
```

The bidding:

SOUTH	WEST	NORTH	EAST
1 ♡	Pass	2 ♣	Pass
3 ♣	Pass	3 ♡	Pass
4 ♡	Pass	Pass	Pass

West may smack his lips over his juicy trump collection, but depression will set in at the end of the hand unless he makes a well-chosen opening lead. Playing for a club ruff is unlikely to be right, for if East has an entry the contract is sure to be defeated anyway. Also, with four trumps, the forcing game is better strategy. Accordingly, West should open the six of diamonds and continue diamonds every time he gains the lead with a high trump. This will give him just enough time to denude declarer of trumps and establish the lowly heart deuce as the setting trick.

PLAYING FOR RUFFS

Like the little boy who enjoys being the only one on his block to own a football, declarer will enjoy life much more if his side is the only one possessing any trumps. He will therefore draw your trumps whenever it is feasible to do so. By making use of your right to play first, however, you may be able to score some ruffing winners before all your trumps have been obliterated. Short-suit leads can be a straightforward and effective way of defeating the contract by paving the way for ruffs, and are especially desirable under the following conditions:

(1)   You feel fairly sure that partner will be able to gain the lead and give you the ruff you seek, either because he has bid and promised some high cards or because your hand is very weak and partner is therefore marked with strength. If you are short in the suit partner has bid, things are particularly favorable, for he is more likely to be able to win the first trick and give you a ruff immediately.

(2)   You have a quick entry in the trump suit and therefore are sure to regain the lead before declarer can finish drawing trumps.

(3)   You have some extra low trumps for ruffing.

(4)   You are desperate, and no other hope is available.

However, tend to avoid short-suit leads when:

(1)   You have no excess low trumps, and your trumps are likely to be winners on power anyway—for example, Q J 3, A Q, K Q 10 8, A J 9 5.

(2)   You have four or more trumps, in which case the forcing game is likely to be preferable.

(3)   Your short suit consists of a singleton or doubleton king or queen. Declarer cannot see your shortness and may lose a finesse to your honor if you leave well enough alone. Of course, if partner has bid the suit or strength in the suit is marked in the dummy by the bidding, the lead becomes more attractive as you are less likely to give anything away.

(4) Your short suit consists of a doubleton in dummy's bid suit. This is usually an extremely poor lead, and rarely accomplishes more than to give declarer a head start at setting up some length winners for discards. In fact, even the doubleton lead in an unbid suit is unlikely to yield a ruff unless you have a quick entry *in trumps*. A singleton is another story, for at least if partner wins the first trick you will get an immediate ruff.

Some examples:

(a)	♠ A 8 3	(b)	♠ K Q 10 6	(c)	♠ A 8 3
	♡ 7		♡ 7		♡ J 9 6 5
	◇ Q 8 6 5 2		◇ Q 8 6 5 2		◇ Q J 9 7
	♣ J 8 4 2		♣ 8 4 2		♣ 7 3

(d)	♠ J 9 3
	♡ K 2
	◇ 7 4 3 2
	♣ 8 5 3 2

The bidding:

OPPONENT	YOU	OPPONENT	PARTNER
1 ♠	Pass	2 ♣	Pass
2 ♠	Pass	3 ♠	Pass
4 ♠	Pass	Pass	Pass

Hand (a) is well suited for the singleton lead. You have excess low trumps to use for ruffing, an entry with the spade ace that will give you the lead before trumps are drawn, and not so much strength that partner is unlikely to be able to gain the lead.

With hand (b), lead the diamond five. Your trumps are likely winners by power, but even if they were four small trumps it would be better to play for the forcing game.

Holding hand (c), lead the queen of diamonds. Don't lead a doubleton when dummy has bid the suit.

With hand (d), things are in desperate shape. The club holding does not inspire confidence, as partner may have a short suit with a few honors that declarer can easily ruff out. Also, any other honors your side holds are in front of the opening bidder's strength, so his finesses are likely to work. Extreme measures are called for, and you should lead the heart king in the hope that partner has either the ace or the queen and a quick trump entry. You don't mind risking the loss of a trick by your lead when it is unlikely to be the trick that gives declarer his contract, and here you don't expect to have much chance to beat the hand unless you get lucky in a hurry.

When a short-suit lead offers a clear-cut method for defeating the contract, it is often best to prefer it to less tangible procedures. For example, suppose you hold

♠ A K 6 5   ♡ 7   ◇ 5 4 3 2   ♣ 6 5 3 2

and the opponents quickly reach game via the auction 1 ♠–3 ♠–4 ♠. With four trumps, it would ordinarily be correct to play for the forcing game, but the minor suits are hardly long or strong enough to induce any ruffing by declarer. You might hit partner with strength in a minor, of course, but you still have to guess which one. The singleton heart is a superior lead, for it will defeat the contract if partner has any reasonably quick entry (such as an ace, or a minor-suit king behind dummy's ace). You will simply win a high trump, lead to partner's entry (which will be easier to find when you can see the dummy) and get your ruff to score the vital fourth trick. The difference in this example is that you can see a clear route to defeating the contract with very little help from partner, and when this happens it is best to follow the simplest approach. With

♠ 8 6 5 3   ♡ 7   ◇ Q J 9 8 6 5   ♣ 3 2

it is not at all clear where your tricks are coming from, so lead the diamond queen and try to bring the dreaded force into action.

Review Quiz

In each of the following problems, the auction proceeds as shown. What is your opening lead?

(1)

NORTH	EAST	SOUTH	WEST
—	—	1 ♠	Pass
2 ◇	Pass	3 ♣	Pass
3 ♠	Pass	4 ♠	Pass
Pass	Pass		

You (West) hold:

♠ 9 8 6   ♡ Q J 9 8 2   ◇ 7 5   ♣ A J 7

(2)

NORTH	EAST	SOUTH	WEST
1 ♣	Pass	1 ♡	Pass
2 ♡	Pass	Pass	Pass

You (West) hold:

♠ Q 8 6   ♡ J 8 4 2   ◇ 8 3   ♣ K Q J 9

(3)

NORTH	EAST	SOUTH	WEST
—	—	1 ♡	Pass
2 ♡	Pass	Pass	Pass

You (West) hold:

♠ A J 6 4   ♡ Q 7 5   ◇ 7 4 2   ♣ K J 4

(4)

NORTH	EAST	SOUTH	WEST
—	—	1 ◇	Double
Pass	Pass	Pass	

You (West) hold:

♠ J 10 9 8   ♡ K Q J 5   ◇ 7   ♣ A K J 3

(5)

NORTH	EAST	SOUTH	WEST
1 ♣	Pass	1 ♠	Pass
3 ♣	Pass	3 ♠	Pass
4 ♠	Pass	Pass	Pass

You (West) hold:

♠ K 8 3   ♡ Q 6 3   ◇ Q 7 5 4 2   ♣ K 8

(6)	NORTH	EAST	SOUTH	WEST
	1 ♣	1 ◇	1 ♠	Pass
	1 NT	Pass	3 ♠	Pass
	4 ♠	Pass	Pass	Pass

You (West) hold:

♠ 8 6 3   ♡ 10 5 2   ◇ Q 9 3   ♣ 9 6 4 3

(7)	NORTH	EAST	SOUTH	WEST
	1 ♣	1 ◇	1 ♡	Pass
	1 ♠	Pass	1 NT	Pass
	2 ♡	Pass	Pass	Pass

You (West) hold:

♠ 8 6 3   ♡ K 2   ◇ Q 9 3   ♣ 9 6 5 4 3

(8)	NORTH	EAST	SOUTH	WEST
	—	—	1 ♠	Pass
	3 ♠	Pass	4 ♠	Pass
	Pass	Pass		

You (West) hold:

♠ 9 5 4   ♡ K Q J 7   ◇ A 8 3   ♣ J 10 8

(9)	NORTH	EAST	SOUTH	WEST
	—	Pass	1 ♠	Pass
	2 ♠	Pass	4 ♠	Pass
	Pass	Pass		

You (West) hold:

♠ 8 5 3   ♡ 7   ◇ 8 6 5 2   ♣ 9 8 7 5 3

(10)

NORTH	EAST	SOUTH	WEST
—	—	1 ♡	Pass
2 ◇	Pass	2 ♡	Pass
4 ♡	Pass	Pass	Pass

You (West) hold:

♠ J 10 8 6 4   ♡ A Q 6   ◇ 7 2   ♣ 8 5 3

(11)

NORTH	EAST	SOUTH	WEST
Pass	Pass	1 ♠	Pass
2 ♠	Pass	4 ♠	Pass
Pass	Pass		

You (West) hold:

♠ K J 7 2   ♡ 6   ◇ K Q 10 8   ♣ 9 5 4 2

(12)

NORTH	EAST	SOUTH	WEST
—	—	1 ♡	Pass
2 ♣	Pass	3 ♣	Pass
3 ♡	Pass	4 ♡	Pass
Pass	Pass		

You (West) hold:

♠ 7 3   ♡ A 6   ◇ A J 4 3   ♣ 10 8 7 4 3

(13)

NORTH	EAST	SOUTH	WEST
—	—	1 ♣	Pass
1 ◇	Pass	1 ♡	Pass
3 ♡	Pass	4 ♡	Pass
Pass	Pass		

You (West) hold:

♠ 9 8 7 3   ♡ A 8 6   ◇ 5   ♣ Q 10 8 4 2

(14)

NORTH	EAST	SOUTH	WEST
—	—	1 ♠	Pass
3 ♠	Pass	4 ♠	Pass
Pass	Pass		

You (West) hold:

♠ A 6 5 3   ♡ 7   ◇ A 4 3 2   ♣ J 4 3 2

(15)

NORTH	EAST	SOUTH	WEST
—	1 NT	2 ♡	Pass
Pass	Pass		

You (West) hold:

♠ Q 8 6   ♡ 8 5   ◇ K 7 4 2   ♣ 10 9 6 3

(16)

NORTH	EAST	SOUTH	WEST
1 ◇	Pass	1 ♡	Pass
3 ◇	Pass	3 ♡	Pass
4 ♡	Pass	Pass	Pass

You (West) hold:

♠ K 8 3   ♡ 8 6 3   ◇ 8 7 4 2   ♣ J 9 5

(17)

NORTH	EAST	SOUTH	WEST
1 ♣	Pass	1 ♡	Pass
2 ♡	Pass	2 NT	Pass
3 ♡	Pass	4 ♡	Pass
Pass	Pass		

You (West) hold:

♠ K 8 3   ♡ 8 6 3   ◇ K 7 4 2   ♣ J 9 5

(18)

NORTH	EAST	SOUTH	WEST
—	—	1 ♠	Pass
1 NT	Pass	2 ♡	Pass
3 ♡	Pass	4 ♡	Pass
Pass	Pass		

You (West) hold:

♠ K J 9   ♡ A K 3   ◇ 8 5   ♣ J 10 9 6 5

(19)	NORTH	EAST	SOUTH	WEST
	—	—	1 ♡	Pass
	2 ◇	Pass	2 ♡	Pass
	3 ♡	Pass	Pass	Pass

You (West) hold:

♠ Q 10 6 4 2   ♡ 7   ◇ A 7 2   ♣ 9 8 4 3

(20)	NORTH	EAST	SOUTH	WEST
	—	—	1 ♡	Pass
	Pass	Pass		

You (West) hold:

♠ K J 8   ♡ 6 4   ◇ K 8 7 3   ♣ 7 5 3 2

(21)	NORTH	EAST	SOUTH	WEST
	Pass	1 ♠	2 ♡	Double
	Pass	Pass	Pass	

You (West) hold:

♠ 8   ♡ K 9 6 5   ◇ A 9 7 4   ♣ J 10 9 3

(22)	NORTH	EAST	SOUTH	WEST
	—	—	1 ◇	Pass
	2 ◇	Pass	3 ◇	Pass
	Pass	Pass		

You (West) hold:

♠ K J 6   ♡ A Q 8 4   ◇ 8 5 3   ♣ J 8 4

(23)	NORTH	EAST	SOUTH	WEST
	—	1 ♡	1 ♠	2 ♡
	2 ♠	Pass	Pass	Pass

You (West) hold:

♠ 8 6 5   ♡ K 7 3 2   ◇ A 10 7   ♣ J 5 3

(24)	NORTH	EAST	SOUTH	WEST
	—	1 ♡	2 ◇	3 ♡
	4 ◇	4 ♡	5 ◇	Pass
	Pass	Double	Pass	Pass
	Pass			

You (West) hold:

♠ K J 3   ♡ A Q 8 6   ◇ 7 4   ♣ K J 8 5

(Your side is vulnerable.)

(25)	NORTH	EAST	SOUTH	WEST
	1 ♣	Pass	1 ◇	Pass
	1 ♠	Pass	2 ♣	Pass
	2 ◇	Pass	3 ◇	Pass
	Pass	Pass		

You (West) hold:

♠ J 7 5   ♡ K 10 8 3   ◇ A 7 4   ♣ 6 5 3

Solutions

(1) *Eight of spades*   Stopping club ruffs in dummy is more important than establishing possible winners in hearts.

(2) *King of clubs*   Even though the suit has been bid by the opponents, your strong holding suggests that clubs is a good place to build tricks and perhaps start a forcing game.

(3) *Seven of diamonds*   Your other suits are unattractive to lead from, so go passive.

(4) *Seven of diamonds*   No choice; partner's pass of a one-level takeout double demands a trump lead.

(5) *Three of hearts*   North has promised a long club suit which will provide discards for South's losers, so you need

to get busy in a hurry. Therefore, lead your shorter unbid suit, which stands a chance of establishing a few tricks. A diamond would be safer, but you cannot afford to play for safety.

(6)   *Queen of diamonds*   Dummy is marked with diamond strength and you have no side entries, so lead the queen of partner's suit rather than the usual small card from three to an honor.

(7)   *Three of diamonds*   This time, declarer is marked with strength in diamonds, and the queen lead could easily cost a trick. Also, you have a probable side entry. Make your normal lead.

(8)   *King of hearts*   The solid sequence offers both safety and the potential establishment of a few tricks at the same time, and there is no reason to suspect that any other suit will be more effective.

(9)   *Seven of hearts*   With such a weak hand, partner is almost certain to have some entries even though he passed originally, so play for the ruff.

(10)   *Jack of spades*   Attack from your nearly solid sequence. The doubleton in dummy's suit is a good lead to avoid.

(11)   *King of diamonds*   Play for the forcing game with four trumps.

(12)   *Three of clubs*   With both opponents bidding clubs, partner can have no more than a singleton and may well be void. The three-spot asks him to return a diamond— the lower-ranking of the two side suits—when he gains the lead by ruffing a club. Your heart ace ensures that declarer cannot draw trumps before some fatal ruffs take place, but even with two small trumps the club lead is still correct.

(13)   *Five of diamonds*   Declarer can't draw trumps in a hurry because of your heart ace, and your hand is weak enough so that partner is reasonably likely to have an entry.

(14)   *Seven of hearts*   Even with four trumps, play for a ruff when it offers the prospects of a sure set. With any one entry in partner's hand, the heart lead beats the contract as you score your two aces, one ruff, and partner's

entry. Besides, the minor-suit holdings are very unattractive to lead from.

(15)   *Five of hearts*   Your side has considerable high-card strength in view of partner's notrump opening, so cut down the enemy's most likely source of winners—ruffs.

(16)   *Three of spades*   You're in desperate trouble in view of North's long diamond suit and your diamond holding. Attack!

(17)   *Six of hearts*   The opponents have staggered into game, and you have no reason to get busy in a hurry.

(18)   *King of hearts*   The bidding suggests that dummy is short in spades, else he would have gone back to declarer's first suit. You can play three rounds of hearts right away and may be able to wipe out all of dummy's ruffing power, thus preserving two spade winners of your own.

(19)   *Four of spades*   Partner may be long in trumps and may welcome a forcing game.

(20)   *Four of hearts*   Partner should usually refuse to let the opponents play a one-level contract unless he is long in trumps, and your heart doubleton and weak hand suggest that this may well be the case here. Thus, your best bet is probably to stop ruffs by the opponents.

(21)   *Eight of spades*   Don't think about solid sequences or forcing declarer when you have a delightful choice like the singleton in partner's suit with an ample supply of trumps.

(22)   *Five of diamonds*   Not an attempt to stop ruffs, but simply the safest lead. The other holdings are too risky to lead from with no clues available from the bidding.

(23)   *Two of hearts*   The normal lead with four or more cards in partner's suit.

(24)   *Four of diamonds*   Your side has plenty of power, and the opponents are apparently hoping that 5 $\diamond$ will be a cheap save against your vulnerable game. There is no hurry to cash winners, so cut down the enemy's most probable source of tricks by leading trumps.

(25)   *Three of hearts*   The bidding so strongly suggests that hearts is a weak spot that the heart lead, while somewhat risky, is justified.

6

Leads Against Slam Contracts

♠ ♡ ◇ ♣

Suppose you are on opening lead with the following hand:

♠ K Q 4 2   ♡ A 6   ◇ 8 4   ♣ 10 9 8 7 4

Against a 3 NT contract, you would lead the club ten and plan to use your high cards in the side suits as entries with which to establish length winners in clubs. If instead the opponents were to play in 4 ♡ and the auction offered no clues, the club ten would be the safest lead; the establishment of one spade trick by leading the king might easily be offset by the gift of a crucial trick to declarer. But suppose the auction proceeds as follows:

OPPONENT	YOU	OPPONENT	PARTNER
1 ♡	Pass	2 ◇	Pass
3 ◇	Pass	4 ♡	Pass
4 NT	Pass	5 ♡	Pass
6 ♡ or 6 NT	Pass	Pass	Pass

The best lead by far is the king of spades. You need only two tricks to defeat the small slam contract, and the bonuses awarded for bidding and making slams are so large that you should always make a one-trick set your primary objective. The spade lead will set up the queen as a probable winner, and your heart ace will provide the necessary entry to cash the setting trick. It would be poor strategy to lead the heart ace first regardless of whether or not hearts are trumps, because you cannot afford to surrender your entry before the crucial second trick is set up.

Unfortunately for the defenders, fate does not usually conspire to deal all the outstanding high cards to the opening leader.

If in the above example your spade queen is replaced by a low spade, you have quite a difficult decision to make. If partner has the spade queen, you want to lead a spade for the same reasons as before; but if partner has no spade honors, the lead away from the king may very well cost a trick (and the slam). The spade is still the recommended choice against a 6 ♡ contract, because the opponents' strong bidding and fit in the diamond suit suggest that you need to take tricks quickly; but against 6 NT you should go passive and lead the club ten. Finally, if both your high spades are replaced by low cards, a spade lead is less risky (though it might help declarer solve a two-way guess for the queen), but it just might be that partner's high cards are in clubs and a club lead is essential to defeat the contract. Against 6 ♡, you should still lead a spade, since you are more likely to avoid declarer's ruffing power by leading the shorter unbid suit and the auction calls for aggressiveness, but against 6 NT safety considerations are paramount and the club ten is the preferred choice. In all of these cases, the absence of a clear route to the two tricks needed to set the contract requires that you make a decision that may turn out to be wrong, and makes it more difficult to find the winning lead. Since these types of hands are the most common, let's look at some principles that will improve the odds in favor of your reaching the winning conclusion.

SMALL SLAMS IN SUITS

Aces represent time as well as power. If the opponents need any tricks in a suit in which you hold the ace, they must permit you to gain the lead, at which time you may be able to cash a winner that you have carefully set up in a different suit. An opening lead of the ace may give declarer the time he needs to make his slam by allowing him to take his tricks in the suit without losing the lead to the defense. It is also possible, however, that if you don't cash your ace, declarer will discard his losers in the suit before you can regain the lead. This will prove particularly embarrassing if partner has the king and you could easily have defeated the slam by taking the first two tricks in the suit;

or if your side has a sure trick which, with your ace, would have defeated the contract.

As the opening leader, you are working with such limited information that it is impossible to guarantee success all of the time, but you will come out well ahead in the long run if you lead your ace against a small slam in a suit *only* under the following conditions:

(1) You have a certain or probable second trick that needs no establishment, such as the king of trumps, and expect to defeat the slam if your ace survives on the first trick; and the suit has not been bid by the opponents.

(2) The bidding suggests that you may be able to take two quick tricks in the suit, because partner has either the king or a void or singleton.

Barring exceptional circumstances, *don't* lead an ace if:

(1) You don't have a quick second trick.
(2) The opponents have bid the suit (unless you are trying for a ruff).
(3) The bidding suggests that an opponent is void in the suit.

Let's look at some examples:

(a)	♠ 10 9 8 4 3	(b)	♠ A 8 3	(c)	♠ 6 3
	♡ 8 7 5		♡ K 9 4		♡ 9 5 2
	◊ A 6		◊ 8 7 4		◊ A 8 7 6
	♣ Q 6 2		♣ J 8 3 2		♣ 6 5 3 2

The bidding:

OPPONENT	YOU	OPPONENT	PARTNER
1 ♡	Pass	2 ◊	Pass
3 ◊	Pass	3 ♡	Pass
4 NT	Pass	5 ◊	Pass
6 ♡	Pass	Pass	Pass

Leading the ace on hand (a) is very poor. The opponents have announced possession of a great many diamonds, and will surely wish to play this suit themselves so as to establish winners and perhaps take discards as well. Lead the club deuce, hoping to find partner with the king so that you can set up a trick quickly before your diamond ace is dislodged. A spade lead could be right, but needs more help from partner.

In example (b), there is a reasonably good chance that your heart king will provide a trick; partner is unlikely to have much in view of your strength, and spades have not been bid by the opponents. Therefore, the lead of the spade ace is reasonable.

On hand (c), both opponents have bid diamonds and you have four of them, so it may very well be that partner has a singleton (or void). Lead the ace and follow with another diamond, hoping that partner can ruff.

(d)   ♠ K 7 4
♡ J 10 9
◇ 8 6
♣ A 8 6 3 2

The bidding:

OPPONENT	YOU	OPPONENT	PARTNER
1 ♠	Pass	2 ◇	Pass
2 ♡	Pass	2 ♠	Pass
4 ◇	Pass	4 ♠	Pass
6 ♠	Pass	Pass	Pass

Here you have a probable trick with the spade king, but the bidding should warn you against an attempt to cash the club ace. Declarer has bid spades, hearts, and jump-supported diamonds, so there isn't much room for clubs in his hand. The complete deal:

NORTH
♠ 10 9 6 5
♡ 7 4
◇ A J 7 3
♣ K Q 5

WEST (you)
♠ K 7 4
♡ J 10 9
◇ 8 6
♣ A 8 6 3 2

EAST
♠ 2
♡ 8 5 3 2
◇ Q 10 9
♣ J 10 9 7 4

SOUTH
♠ A Q J 8 3
♡ A K Q 6
◇ K 5 4 2
♣ —

The ace of clubs lead hands South his slam, for he simply ruffs and discards two low diamonds on dummy's high clubs. If, however, you make the safe lead of the jack of hearts, declarer will lose one spade trick and one diamond trick.

(e)   ♠ 6 5 3
♡ 7 4 2
◇ J 3 2
♣ A 7 6 5

The bidding:

OPPONENT	YOU	OPPONENT	PARTNER
1 ♠	Pass	3 ♠	Pass
6 ♠	Pass	Pass	Pass

On this auction, just about anything could be happening. South could be gambling on a favorable lead; the opponents could have concealed strength in clubs. When you encounter "jumpy" auctions like this, the quality of the opponents becomes very important. If they are weak players or "wild" bidders, the ace lead is reasonable; you may be able to cash the first two tricks in this suit if declarer has misbid or has gambled on a favorable lead. A good player, however, will usually not jump to 6 ♠ without first- or second-round control in the unbid suit, so lead the heart seven if you trust declarer's bidding.

If you don't have an ace, you should still be willing to risk leading away from a queen to try and build up a trick if partner has the king, for he may have the vital second trick. Whether or not to gamble on leading away from a king, however, depends on the bidding. If you are likely to need tricks in a hurry and the king is in an unbid suit, the risk may be worthwhile; but if an opponent has bid the suit, or the bidding indicates no special urgency about taking tricks, go passive and hope to score the king as a result of a losing finesse by declarer. Remember that if an opponent promises strength in the suit by bidding notrump, this is in effect the same as if he had bid the suit. For example, suppose you are faced with the following situation:

OPPONENT	YOU	OPPONENT	PARTNER
1 ♡	Pass	2 ◇	Pass
2 NT	Pass	4 ♡	Pass
6 ♡	Pass	Pass	Pass

You hold:

♠ K 8 5 3   ♡ K 7 3   ◇ 8 6 3   ♣ 10 9 8

Declarer's 2 NT bid promises strength in the unbid suits, so a spade lead should be avoided. Lead the ten of clubs; any club honors partner may hold are in front of declarer and subject to finesses anyway.

As we have seen, solid sequences offer safety as well as trick-taking power, and are therefore often desirable to lead from. If, for example, your spades on the previous hand had been K Q J 9 or J 10 9 8, you would be quite happy to lead your top spade. Even with K Q 7 6, the spade king lead would be justified because of your potential second trick with the heart king.

Singletons are often effective leads against slam contracts. If partner has the ace, the slam is immediately defeated when you ruff the next trick. The slam will also go down if partner has a quick trump entry and can give you your ruff before trumps are drawn. However, tend not to lead a singleton if you have so much high-card strength that partner is unlikely to gain the lead, if both opponents have bid the suit and you may help declarer avoid losing a trick to a bad break, or if you have a sure trick and any trick in partner's hand will defeat the slam without need of a ruff. Some examples:

(a)	♠ 8 6 5	(b)	♠ A 6 3
	♡ 7		♡ 8
	◇ 7 5 3		◇ Q J 10 3
	♣ 8 6 5 4 3 2		♣ 7 5 4 3 2

The bidding:

OPPONENT	YOU	OPPONENT	PARTNER
1 ♠	Pass	3 ♠	Pass
4 NT	Pass	5 ♠	Pass
6 ♠	Pass	Pass	Pass

The singleton heart is a good lead on hand (a). If partner can win the first trick or an early round of trumps, the slam will be defeated, and he is likely to have some strength in view of your miserable holding. On hand (b), however, your ace of trumps ensures that the contract will be defeated if partner can also win a trick, so a ruff is unnecessary. A heart lead may help declarer avoid a loser in the suit, and make his slam, by pinpointing any missing honors in partner's hand. There is absolutely no reason to take this risk. Even if the heart lead sets up a winner in partner's hand, you will have no hearts left to lead after winning the ace of trumps; and you have a lead that is both safe and constructive. Lead the queen of diamonds.*

* Did you question the possibility of partner's winning a trick because you have seven high-card points? Good! You're doing very well. Remember, however, that suit contracts are usually based on distribution as well as high-card strength. If, for example, each opponent is counting two

Trump leads are rarely advisable against small slams, for the defense is unlikely to have enough entries to repeat the process often enough to annoy declarer. However, you should lead a trump if the bidding strongly indicates that declarer will need ruffs in dummy; dummy is likely to be fairly short in trumps, and your holding is safe to lead from (such as two or three small).

6 NT CONTRACTS

There are two main kinds of 6 NT contracts. One is bid on balanced power, where the opponents have no long suits and expect to make the slam primarily on high-card strength. A typical auction would be 1 NT–6 NT. In this situation, go passive in almost all instances. Unless you can see a sure way to develop two tricks or have a solid sequence, getting busy will only help declarer. After all, your high-card winners are unlikely to disappear, as declarer lacks the discarding power available in suit contracts. Moreover, the opponents should not be counting any points for distribution and should therefore have most of the high-card strength, so a lead away from an unsupported honor is likely to be fatal. Sometimes, however, the opponents may play 6 NT as the least of evils, as in the following situation:

NORTH	SOUTH
1 ♢	1 ♠
3 ♢	3 ♡
4 ♢	4 ♡
6 ♢	6 NT
Pass	

This hardly qualifies as the most inspired auction of the year, but you are still faced with the necessity of defeating the

---

points for a singleton, only 29 high-card points will provide the total of 33 needed for slam. Hence, partner *could* hold as much as four high-card points (or even more if the opponents' hands are very distributional).

contract. Holding

♠ 7 6 3   ♡ 8 4 3   ◇ A 4 3 2   ♣ Q 8 7

you should lead the seven of clubs. Any spade or heart honors held by your side are in front of declarer's strength and can be finessed, and North's long diamond suit will surely be set up after your ace is knocked out. Matters are desperate and you should gamble on finding the club king in partner's hand. Change the club queen to the king and a club lead, while more risky, is still correct. This is similar to the situation in a suit contract where you fear that, given time, the opponents can run enough tricks and/or discard their losers on side-suit winners, so you must strike quickly. More often than not, however, passive leads from suits in which you do *not* hold honors will be best against 6 NT contracts.

GRAND SLAMS

Grand slams do not occur frequently enough to warrant extensive discussion of how to lead against them. Most bridge players, save for the experts, are loath to risk squandering the bonus for small slam by going down one in a grand slam, and consequently refuse to contract for a grand slam unless they hold about nineteen cold tricks in the two hands. However, a few points are worth noting:

(1)   When in doubt, go passive. You only need one trick to defeat the slam, so building up winners is unnecessary; if you get on lead to cash them you've already beaten the slam. Thus, your main objective is not to help declarer.

(2)   Trump leads are often very good against grand slams, assuming of course that your trump holding is not dangerous to lead away from. They have the advantage of being passive and at the same time offer the potential of depriving declarer of a needed ruff. In a grand slam, even one less ruff than declarer expects may be fatal.

(3)   As usual, listening to the bidding is essential. Here's an example of the brilliancies that can be produced by an opening leader with a keen ear and sharp powers of deduction:

NORTH	SOUTH
1 ♠	3 ♦
4 ♠	4 NT
5 ♡	5 NT
6 ♦	7 NT
Pass	

You (West) hold:

♠ K 6   ♡ 9 6 3   ♦ J 6 4 2   ♣ 8 7 6 3

What is your lead?

North's unusual jump to 4 ♠ after partner's jump shift marks him with a solid spade suit, except for the king which you can see in your own hand. South may not have more than a singleton spade, but this is unlikely to matter in view of your doubleton, for your king will drop on the second lead of the suit. Thus, the spades will run—but the diamonds will not, for South should have the top honors in the suit and your jack will serve as a stopper. You can predict in advance how the play will go after a neutral lead such as a club: Declarer will win, cash the ace, king, and queen of diamonds, and look annoyed when you turn up with a stopper. He'll then have to risk his grand slam on the spade situation, and you know that this will work out very well for him. Can anything be done about this? Lead the six of spades!

The complete deal:

```
                    NORTH
                    ♠ A Q J 10 5 4 2
                    ♡ K 7
                    ◇ 8
                    ♣ A 10 9
WEST (you)                           EAST
♠ K 6                                ♠ 9 8 3
♡ 9 6 3                              ♡ J 10 8 5 4 2
◇ J 6 4 2                            ◇ 7
♣ 8 7 6 3                            ♣ 5 4 2
                    SOUTH
                    ♠ 7
                    ♡ A Q
                    ◇ A K Q 10 9 5 3
                    ♣ K Q J
```

Without a good peek, South cannot possibly risk his grand slam by taking the spade finesse at the first trick when any reasonable diamond split will give him thirteen tricks. He will win your spade lead with the ace, and the grand slam will be defeated. On any other lead, he has time to test diamonds and then finesse spades when the diamonds fail to cooperate, which will give him more than enough tricks.

Review Quiz

For each of the following problems, the auction proceeds as shown. What is your opening lead?

(1)	NORTH	EAST	SOUTH	WEST
	—	—	1 ♠	Pass
	3 ♠	Pass	4 ◇	Pass
	4 ♡	Pass	4 ♠	Pass
	5 ◇	Pass	5 ♠	Pass
	6 ♠	Pass	Pass	Pass

You (West) hold:

♠ 6 4 3   ♡ 7 5 2   ◇ 8 6 3   ♣ A 7 4 2

(2)	NORTH	EAST	SOUTH	WEST
	1 ◇	Pass	1 ♠	Pass
	3 ♣	Pass	3 ♠	Pass
	4 ♣	Pass	4 NT	Pass
	5 ◇	Pass	6 NT	Pass
	Pass	Pass		

You (West) hold:

♠ 7 3 2   ♡ Q 10 7 4   ◇ 8 6 3   ♣ 8 5 2

(3)	NORTH	EAST	SOUTH	WEST
	—	—	1 ♡	Pass
	2 ♣	Pass	3 ♣	Pass
	4 ♡	Pass	5 ◇	Pass
	6 ♡	Pass	Pass	Pass

You (West) hold:

♠ 9 8 7 2   ♡ 7 4 2   ◇ 7 6 5 3 2   ♣ 7

(4)	NORTH	EAST	SOUTH	WEST
	—	—	1 ♠	Pass
	3 ♠	Pass	6 ♠	Pass
	Pass	Pass		

You (West) hold:

♠ 8 5   ♡ A K 7 4   ◇ 8 5 3   ♣ J 10 9 7

(5)	NORTH	EAST	SOUTH	WEST
	—	—	1 NT	Pass
	4 NT	Pass	6 NT	Pass
	Pass	Pass		

You (West) hold:

♠ Q 8 6 3   ♡ K 7 4   ◇ 8 5 3   ♣ J 7 4

(6)	NORTH	EAST	SOUTH	WEST
	—	—	1 ♡	Pass
	2 ◇	Pass	2 ♠	Pass
	4 ♠	Pass	6 ♠	Pass
	Pass	Pass		

You (West) hold:

♠ 9 8 3   ♡ 10 9 4 3   ◇ Q 8 6 5 3   ♣ 7

(7)	NORTH	EAST	SOUTH	WEST
	—	—	1 ♡	Pass
	2 ♣	Pass	3 ♣	Pass
	3 ♡	Pass	4 NT	Pass
	5 ♡	Pass	6 ♡	Pass
	Pass	Pass		

You (West) hold:

♠ 8 5 2   ♡ A 6   ◇ J 10 9 3   ♣ 7 4 3 2

(8)	NORTH	EAST	SOUTH	WEST
	—	—	1 ♡	Pass
	3 ♡	Pass	4 NT	Pass
	5 ♡	Pass	6 ♡	Pass
	Pass	Pass		

You (West) hold:

♠ Q 8 4 3   ♡ 6 5 2   ◇ A 7 3   ♣ 10 6 4

(9)	NORTH	EAST	SOUTH	WEST
	—	—	1 ♠	Pass
	2 ◇	Pass	2 ♠	Pass
	3 ♡	Pass	3 NT	Pass
	4 ♠	Pass	6 ♠	Pass
	Pass	Pass		

You (West) hold:

♠ 5 3   ♡ K 7 5 3   ♢ 7 6 3   ♣ 10 8 7 4

(10)	NORTH	EAST	SOUTH	WEST
	1 ♢	Pass	2 ♡	Pass
	3 ♢	Pass	3 ♡	Pass
	4 ♡	Pass	6 ♡	Pass
	Pass	Pass		

You (West) hold:

♠ A 6 3   ♡ Q 10 8   ♢ 7 5 3   ♣ 10 9 8 2

Solutions

(1)   *Ace of clubs* The point of this example is to stress that it is losing strategy always to assume that your opponents bid perfectly. Here, the opponents have cue-bid the red suits and are clearly worried about clubs; North may have gone on to 6 ♠ because he has second-round control of clubs or simply because he felt silly playing in the unusual contract of 5 ♠. The lead is unlikely to cost, for if South had the king of clubs he probably would have bid 6 ♠ (or 5 NT) instead of 5 ♠.

(2)   *Four of hearts* The opponents appear to be playing notrump by default rather than by choice, and a heart lead may set up a vital trick in a hurry. Incidentally, 4 NT in this sequence should not be treated as Blackwood, but opponents do not always follow the correct bidding methods.

(3)   *Nine of spades* Don't lead a singleton when both opponents have bid the suit; attack in the unbid suit.

(4)   *King of hearts* Perhaps the first or second round of hearts will be ruffed, but why be pessimistic?

(5)   *Eight of diamonds* Go passive against "balanced" notrump slams.

(6) *Seven of clubs* The ruff is the most likely method for defeating the contract. Either South or East is likely to have a singleton diamond, and neither eventuality will help you even if East has the king.

(7) *Two of clubs* With both opponents bidding clubs, play to give partner a ruff. You will lead another club when you win your ace of trumps.

(8) *Three of spades* Even though diamonds have not been bid, the best strategy is still to try and build up a winner in spades before your diamond ace is knocked out. You have no reason to suspect that declarer can discard all of his diamonds on a side suit—or even that he wants to.

(9) *Three of hearts* Hope to build up a trick if partner has the queen. Any strength in hearts is marked in dummy on the bidding, so the lead is unlikely to cost. Declarer has promised strength in clubs, so any club honors partner has can probably be finessed, and South is therefore unlikely to need many club ruffs in dummy. As it happens, a club or trump lead will give declarer time to discard his losing hearts on a side suit and make the slam.

(10) *Ace of spades* South is marked with just about all of the heart strength on the bidding, so your heart queen is a probable winner. Therefore, try and grab your spade ace. Even if the heart strength appeared to be more evenly divided, the ace lead would still be reasonable as North would need both a high heart honor and the jack to deprive you of a trump winner.

7

Lead–Directing Doubles

♠   ♡   ◇   ♣

One of life's more pleasant (albeit infrequent) situations is to hold a suit such as ◇ A K Q J 7 5 and hear the opponents' bidding proceed 1 NT–3 NT. That is, the situation is delightful provided that you are on opening lead and can run your six winners without delay. If partner is on lead, however, matters may become extremely irritating, for he may unimaginatively produce the fourth-best card from his longest suit (which is most unlikely to be diamonds) and declarer may cash nine tricks and make his contract before you can regain the lead. Anything is better than this horrendous calamity, so let's look at some methods which you might use to avert this disaster:

(1)   You can say to partner, "Lead a diamond." This will obtain the desired lead, but will also result in permanent ostracism by the opponents (plus any other bridge players who happen to be on the premises).

(2)   You can arrange a special code word with partner, such as "yaphrax," to alert him to the necessity for an unusual lead without telling him what suit you want. Unfortunately, a bidding sequence such as

OPPONENT	PARTNER	OPPONENT	YOU
1 NT	Pass	3 NT	Yaphrax

while highly imaginative, is also completely illegal.

(3)   You can bid 4 ◇ over 3 NT. This has the advantage of being one hundred percent legal, but entails a small problem. You will be required to play the hand in 4 ◇ (undoubtedly doubled), and partner will never get the opportunity to lead against (and defeat) the 3 NT contract.

(4)   You can double 3 NT. Here, at last, is a potentially sane solution. The double is perfectly legal; the opponents are still required to play the hand; and you will collect a larger penalty if partner does in fact lead a diamond. There are risks, however. Partner may misunderstand the meaning of your double and fail to lead a diamond, allowing the opponents to make their contract and score a substantial bonus. Or, the double may warn the opponents about the necessity of escaping from the dangerous 3 NT contract, and they may run out to a suit contract which you cannot defeat.

A similar situation arises if partner is on opening lead against a suit contract, you are void in a side suit, and you fear that partner will lead a different suit unless something drastic is done to alert him to the need for special action (i.e., giving you a ruff). One possible way of making partner sit up and take notice is to double the final contract. However, again the opponents will reap extra dividends if they make their contract, either because partner misinterprets your message or because you cannot beat the hand even with the ruff. Also, the double may chase the opponents into a contract you cannot defeat.

As you can see, doubling the final contract to direct partner to a particular lead must be done with care, but can be an extremely useful weapon provided that:

(1)   You are reasonably certain that the lead which you direct by doubling will set the contract, and you fear that partner will make some other lead that is likely to be harmful to the defense unless you double.

(2)   The meaning of the double is clear, and partner will know what is expected of him. It must be remembered that a double can be lead-directional *only* when the penalty interpretation is not a reasonable one. (See below.)

(3)   The opponents are not likely to escape to a contract of equal or greater importance which you cannot defeat. (Chasing the opponents out of a game contract that they would have made with partner's probable lead into a cold part-score contract, however, represents a gain.)

In addition to doubling the final contract, it is sometimes possible to double earlier in the auction to suggest a lead. A fairly large number of bids, such as Stayman and the response to

Blackwood, are artificial. Therefore, you can call attention to the specific suit you want led by doubling the artificial bid—provided, of course, that your right-hand opponent bids the suit you desire. The opponents will usually be unable to play the contract in the artificial bid, so you do not risk having to pay out any extra points if the opponents make the hand. However, even this clever scheme is not without its disadvantages. First, the right suit must be bid by the right opponent so you can double. Second, the double allows the next player two useful extra bids, "redouble" and "pass," to describe his strength in the suit. Third, if your requested lead proves helpful to declarer, partner will be most unhappy. So do not go gaily doubling in all situations, but reserve this useful bid for times when you feel the lead you want is likely to be necessary to defeat the contract.

Now that we have considered the two basic types of lead-directing doubles, let's shift back across the table and confront the situations as they will appear to you when you are on opening lead.

DOUBLES AFTER 1 NT–3 NT

Suppose the auction proceeds:

OPPONENT	YOU	OPPONENT	PARTNER
1 NT	Pass	3 NT	Double
Pass	Pass	Pass	

Experience has shown that it is losing strategy to double the 3 NT bid simply because of an impressive number of high-card points. Declarer's task is always much easier when the defensive strength is concentrated in one hand, especially when he is alerted to this fact by the double. Declarer knows which finesses will win and which will lose, and the doubler is constantly being subjected to such indignities as endplays (because his partner can never gain the lead), squeezes (because he holds all the high cards, and the opponents must have tricks somewhere—probably a long suit), and writing down large numbers on the enemy's side of the score sheet (because of his foolish double). Therefore, the best strategy when holding a hand with a great deal of high-card strength and no long suit to run is to lie low and *pass*. Declarer will probably misread the lack of bidding and go down because he does not expect one hand (yours) to have so many points.

Presuming, then, that partner knows what he's doing and doubles a 3 NT contract, your best bet is to lead your *shortest* suit—for the odds favor that that's where partner's length and strength are located. (For the double, partner should hold a five-card or longer suit to the A K Q J or a five-card or longer suit to the K Q J 10 and a side ace.) For example, lead the nine of clubs from:

♠ 10 9 8 7 ♡ K 8 5 ◇ 9 7 6 2 ♣ 9 3

DOUBLES OF 3 NT CONTRACTS*

Doubles of 3 NT contracts reached by auctions other than 1 NT–3 NT usually have some lead-directional implications, though the doubler's basic goal may be to increase the penalty.

If your side has not bid, a double usually suggests the lead of the suit first bid by dummy. However, this is not a unilateral command. For example:

(a)	OPPONENT	YOU	OPPONENT	PARTNER
	—	—	1 ♠	Pass
	1 NT	Pass	2 NT	Pass
	3 NT	Pass	Pass	Double
	Pass	Pass	Pass	

(b)	OPPONENT	YOU	OPPONENT	PARTNER
	—	—	1 ◇	Pass
	1 ♡	Pass	1 ♠	Pass
	1 NT	Pass	2 NT	Pass
	3 NT	Pass	Pass	Double
	Pass	Pass	Pass	

* The methods described in this section also apply to 1 NT and 2 NT contracts. These doubles are less advisable, however, because of the risk of doubling the opponents into game.

(c)	OPPONENT	YOU	OPPONENT	PARTNER
	—	—	1 ♣	Pass
	1 ♠	Pass	2 ♣	Pass
	2 ♡	Pass	3 ♣	Pass
	3 NT	Pass	Pass	Double
	Pass	Pass	Pass	

On auction (a), partner's double strongly suggests a spade lead. If he had a good suit of his own, he might have bid it over 1 ♠.

In case (b), a diamond is likely to be a good choice if you have no clear-cut lead, though a very attractive selection such as Q J 10 9 8 should be preferred.

In sequence (c), however, a club lead is pointless, for dummy is marked with great length in the suit. Partner surely has some club stoppers behind dummy for his double, but declarer will probably want to play the suit himself to set up some length-winners. Go after your own suits; the auction suggests that a diamond lead is likely to work well.

If only partner has bid, a double of 3 NT demands that you lead his suit. You must follow orders unless you are void.

If only you have bid, a double of 3 NT demands that you lead your own suit. Partner is afraid you may decide not to do so in view of the opponents' notrump bids, and strongly believes that the lead of your suit will defeat the contract. His most likely holding is a high card in your suit plus a sure entry in the opponents' long suit.

If both you and your partner have bid, lead your own suit. This is somewhat more debatable than the preceding rules, and you should discuss this situation in advance with your partner to be sure you are playing it the same way. The recommended treatment is based on the principle that you would tend to lead partner's suit rather than your own without the double (if only for the reason that you could yell at him if the lead went wrong, whereas if you led your own suit and were wrong you would be on the receiving end).

DOUBLES OF STAYMAN BIDS

If the bidding proceeds

OPPONENT	YOU	OPPONENT	PARTNER
1 NT	Pass	2 ♣	Double

and 2 ♣ is the Stayman convention, some experts treat the double
as showing strength and length in clubs and requesting a club
lead against whatever contract the opponents play. Not all agree
with this treatment, though it does have the merit of simplicity. If
you choose to use it, however, be sure to have very good clubs
when you double (such as K Q J 8 6 5), or else the opponents
may redouble and make the contract in spite of a short trump
holding because of their many high cards.

DOUBLES OF CUE-BIDS

If the opponents are cue-bidding merrily in an attempt to
reach slam, partner can often send up a flare as to the best lead
by inserting a judicious double. For example:

OPPONENT	YOU	OPPONENT	PARTNER
1 ♠	Pass	3 ♠	Pass
4 ♣	Pass	4 ◇	Double
4 ♠	Pass	6 ♠	Pass
Pass	Pass		

The 4 ◇ bid is not an attempt to play the hand in diamonds,
but is intended to help the opponents investigate their slam
chances and presumably shows the ace or another important
feature. Partner can tell that the most likely result of the auction
is a spade contract, in which case you will be on lead. It is pointless to play this double for penalties, for 4 ◇ is very unlikely to

be the final contract; so partner must be asking you to lead a diamond. He should have a strong holding, such as K Q 10 8 3, in this suit.

This double can be very useful if it is not abused. Partner should *not* double 4 ◇ with

♠ 7 6 3   ♡ K 8 5   ◇ K 7 3   ♣ 8 6 4 2

For all he knows, a heart may be the killing lead. Change the heart king to a small heart and the double is still incorrect, for a heart lead could easily be right (you might have the king-queen, and declarer could be hoping to discard hearts on dummy's diamonds). Thus, the double should be made only when a particular lead is strongly desired.

Another good time not to double a cue-bid is when the opponents may choose to play the doubled contract. Don't commit the mortifying error that an opponent of mine once made:

SOUTH	WEST	NORTH	EAST
1 ◇	Pass	1 ♡	Pass
4 ♡	Pass	5 ♣	Pass
5 ◇	Double	Pass	Pass
Redouble!	Pass	Pass	Pass

West wanted a diamond lead (which he would ruff) against a 5 ♡ or 6 ♡ contract, and he was right; the diamond lead would result in a set. Unfortunately, the bidding never got that far, for as South I held ◇ A Q J 10 4 3 and was more than willing to play the cold redoubled game in the suit in which I had opened the bidding.

DOUBLES OF BLACKWOOD RESPONSES

A new suit bid in response to the Blackwood convention is similar to a cue-bid in that the opponents are unlikely to want to play in that suit. Therefore, partner can double with impunity if he strongly desires the lead. For example:

SOUTH	WEST (you)	NORTH	EAST
1 ♡	Pass	3 ♡	Pass
4 NT	Pass	5 ◊	Double
6 ♡	Pass	Pass	Pass

East knows that the opponents are not going to play in 5 ◊ after locating the heart fit. Thus, the double must be intended to call your attention to the desirability of a diamond lead, and you should follow partner's suggestion, barring some strong reason to the contrary.

As was the case with Sherlock Holmes' oft-discussed dog in the nighttime, partner's doing nothing may be significant:

SOUTH	WEST (you)	NORTH	EAST
1 ♡	Pass	2 ♣	Pass
3 ♡	Pass	4 ♡	Pass
4 NT	Pass	5 ◊	Pass
6 ♡	Pass	Pass	Pass

Holding:

♠ 9 8 3   ♡ K 8 6   ◊ 9 8 3   ♣ 7 5 4 2

lead the spade nine. You hope to hit partner's strength before discards are taken on the clubs, and his failure to double 5 ◊ suggests that you look elsewhere for his values.

DOUBLES OF SLAM CONTRACTS

Doubling a slam contract simply to increase the penalty is losing strategy, for several reasons. First of all, the opponents are unlikely to go down more than one trick in view of their great power. Therefore, you stand to gain only 50 or 100 points by your double, and are risking the loss of several hundred points if the opponents make their contract—and even more if they re-double. Second, if you double a suit slam on high-card strength, such as two aces or ace-king in a side suit, the opponents may well turn up with a critical void or singleton and easily make their contract. Third, the information given declarer by the double will often help him find the play that saves the contract. Fourth, the double will cost well over a thousand points if the opponents take heed and run to a different slam which they can make. You should not double a 6 ♡ contract even with

♠ 8 5 3   ♡ Q J 10 9   ◇ 8 7 6   ♣ 8 4 3

because the opponents may run to 6 NT and be able to cash twelve tricks, nor should you double in the following situation:

SOUTH	WEST	NORTH	EAST
1 ♡	Pass	3 ♣	Pass
3 ♡	Pass	4 ♣	Pass
4 NT	Pass	5 ♡	Pass
6 NT	?		

West holds:

♠ 8 5 2   ♡ 7 6 3   ◇ A K 2   ♣ 6 5 3 2

West is certain to defeat 6 NT, and therefore doubled when the hand was actually held. South, being no fool, realized that his side had committed a faux pas in the bidding and ran out to 7 ♣, which had the advantage of placing East on lead. East knew his partner had tricks in one of the unbid suits, but had no way of telling which one. After long minutes of agonized thought he unfortunately chose to lead a spade, and the opponents were able to run off thirteen tricks. West's arithmetical talent was sadly lacking; in order to try and increase the penalty from 50 to 100 points, he handed the opponents a 1,440-point bonanza.

A much better strategy is to double a slam contract in order to obtain a particular lead which you think is essential to defeat the slam. Now you stand to gain not just 50 or 100 points but the entire value of the slam that the opponents will be prevented from making. The procedure used by most experts is the one invented by Theodore Lightner, which has come to be known (with no great originality) as the Lightner double. This double asks for an unusual lead—one that would not have been made without the

double. The most frequent meaning is that the doubler is void of
a suit and wishes to ruff, so you should consider your longest non-
trump suit for your lead. Do *not* lead any suit bid by partner
or any suit unbid by the opponents, for these are normal leads
that you would be likely to make without the double. Tend not
to lead a suit you have bid unless it is very long and you think
partner wants to ruff. If you have no long suit and are in doubt,
lead the first non-trump suit bid by dummy. Some examples:

(a)	OPPONENT	YOU	OPPONENT	PARTNER
	1 ♡	Pass	3 ♡	Pass
	4 NT	Pass	5 ♡	Pass
	6 ♡	Pass	Pass	Double
	Pass	Pass	Pass	

You hold:

♠ 9 8 7   ♡ 6   ◊ 8 7 6 4 3 2   ♣ K Q J

Lead a diamond (the deuce, since you would like partner
to return the lower-ranking side suit if he ruffs).
The complete deal:

DUMMY
♠ A Q J
♡ 10 9 3 2
◊ A Q 5
♣ 10 9 5

YOU
♠ 9 8 7
♡ 6
◊ 8 7 6 4 3 2
♣ K Q J

PARTNER
♠ 10 6 5 4 2
♡ A 7 4
◊ —
♣ 8 6 4 3 2

SOUTH
♠ K 3
♡ K Q J 8 5
◊ K J 10 9
♣ A 7

Partner correctly gambled that the opponents would not or could not run out to 6 NT. Without the double, you would lead the club king and declarer would happily play three rounds of spades and discard his low club, drive out the heart ace, draw trumps, and wrap up the slam.

(b)	OPPONENT	YOU	OPPONENT	PARTNER
	1 ◇	Pass	1 ♠	Pass
	3 ◇	Pass	4 ◇	Pass
	6 ◇	Pass	Pass	Double
	Pass	Pass		

You hold:

♠ 9 7 5   ♡ 8 6 3   ◇ 7 4 2   ♣ 10 9 8 5

Lead the nine of spades. The opponents would surely have bid clubs if partner were void, since you have only four, so the longest unbid suit should be rejected in favor of the first side suit bid by dummy.

(c)	SOUTH	WEST	NORTH	EAST
	—	—	1 ♣	Pass
	1 ♠	Pass	3 ♠	Pass
	4 NT	Pass	5 ◇	Pass
	5 NT	Pass	6 ◇	Pass
	6 ♠	Pass	Pass	Double
	Redouble	Pass	Pass	Pass

You (West) hold:

♠ 7   ♡ K 9 6 5   ◇ K 10 7 4   ♣ K 9 8 2

This deal was reported by Sonny Moyse in the July 1961 *Bridge World,* and the lead made a difference of a mere 3,620 points! East can't want a diamond lead, as he had two chances to double diamond responses to Blackwood bids, and a heart (the unbid suit) would be the usual lead. East must want dummy's first-bid suit—clubs. Let's see what happened after the lead of a low club:

NORTH
♠ K Q J 6
♡ J 8 7
◇ Q
♣ A Q J 7 3

WEST   EAST
♠ 7   ♠ 5 4 2
♡ K 9 6 5   ♡ 10 4 3 2
◇ K 10 7 4   ◇ J 9 6 5 3 2
♣ K 9 8 2   ♣ —

SOUTH
♠ A 10 9 8 3
♡ A Q
◇ A 8
♣ 10 6 5 4

South could have made the slam by simply playing low from dummy at trick one and later discarding the heart queen on dummy's long club, but he was not knowledgeable about Lightner doubles and put up the ace "in case the lead was a singleton." This is nonsense, of course, since East wouldn't have the semblance of a double with just a king or two, but it proved quite profitable to the defense. East ruffed and returned a heart, and South desperately finessed in an attempt to hold his losses to down one. West won, cashed the club king, and gave East another ruff —down 1600 (North-South were vulnerable). Admittedly, declarer's bad play was primarily responsible for the failure to score 2,020 points by making 6 ♠ redoubled, and the double was highly risky since the contract was in fact makable, but who can argue with success?

OPPONENT	YOU	OPPONENT	PARTNER
1 ♡	Pass	3 ♡	Pass
4 ♣	Pass	4 ♡	Pass
6 ♡	Pass	Pass	Double
Pass	Pass	Pass	

You hold:

♠ 8 6 5   ♡ 7 3   ◊ 10 9 8 6   ♣ 7 6 5 4

Can you deduce the unusual lead in this instance? Either of the unbid suits would be relatively normal, so partner must want you to lead declarer's bid suit. Lead the seven of clubs.

While partner will often make a Lightner double to indicate that he is void in a suit and wishes to ruff the opening lead, his failure to double does not necessarily indicate that he has no voids. He may fear that the double will encourage the opponents to run out to a contract that cannot be defeated, and rely on the hope that you will find the right opening lead without any help. An example of this principle occurred in the 1968 World Team Olympiad in Deauville, France, where the United States women's team scored a handsome gain on the following deal:

<pre>
                    NORTH
                    ♠ 7 6
                    ♡ A 2
                    ◊ K J 10 4
                    ♣ Q 9 7 5 4
     WEST   EAST
     ♠ 10 9   ♠ 8 4 2
     ♡ Q J 10 9 7 6 5 4 3   ♡ —
     ◊ 6 5   ◊ 9 8 7 3 2
     ♣ —   ♣ K J 10 8 3
                    SOUTH
                    ♠ A K Q J 5 3
                    ♡ K 8
                    ◊ A Q
                    ♣ A 6 2
</pre>

The bidding:

SOUTH	WEST	NORTH	EAST
2 ♣	5 ♡	6 ♡	Pass
7 ♠	Pass	Pass	Pass

East feared that a double of 7 ♠ might induce the opponents to escape to 7 NT, which in fact is ironclad. Also, she felt that West might well lead her own suit in any event. However, West decided that East's failure to double denied a void and led the diamond six, and the American South claimed the contract.

When the deal was replayed with the American team holding the East-West cards, the opponents reached only 6 ♠, which East also refused to double for fear of the notrump escape. This time, however, West led a heart—the three-spot, requesting a club return. East ruffed and returned a low club, West ruffed South's ace, and the contract went down four.

East was correct in judging that she could not afford to make a Lightner double, and West should have led a heart in spite of East's final pass. Also, note that if East did in fact double and the opponents failed to run, the nine-card suit should make it quite clear what suit East wants led. The fact that West has bid the suit and it is not truly an "unusual" lead is immaterial. (A nine-card suit is in and of itself unusual.)

DOUBLES OF SLAM CONTRACTS: SOME ADVANCED SITUATIONS

On occasion, you will wish to double an opponent's cue-bid with strength in the suit even though you are on opening lead, in order to help partner with the defense. If partner then doubles the final contract, he wants you to lead the suit you have doubled. For example:

SOUTH	WEST (you)	NORTH	EAST
—	—	1 ♣	Pass
1 ♦	Pass	1 ♠	Pass
2 NT	Pass	3 ♣	Pass
4 ♣	Pass	4 NT	Pass
5 ♡	Double	6 NT	Double
Pass	Pass	Pass	

You (West) hold:

♠ 8 7 2   ♡ K J 9 3   ◇ 9 6 3   ♣ 6 4 2

This problem was submitted to a panel of experts in the April 1967 *Bridge World,* and the principle is apparently not a straightforward one. The heart lead was the most popular, but was endorsed by only 21 of the 42 panelists. This simply demonstrates that opening leads are difficult even for experts, for West is unlikely to lead a heart without the double in view of South's jump to 2 NT and East's most probable holding is a heart honor and a likely trick somewhere else.

The next problem was presented to an expert panel in the November–December 1966 *Bridge Journal.* Only 8 of 35 panelists found the winning lead (though many agreed later with the reasoning); can you do better?

OPPONENT	YOU	OPPONENT	PARTNER
—	—	1 ♡	Pass
1 ♠	2 ◇	3 ♠	Pass
4 ◇	Pass	5 ♣	Double
6 ♠	Pass	Pass	Double
Pass	Pass	Pass	

Assuming that you have no obvious long suit to lead, what suit are you asked to lead? (Remember, a slam should not be doubled to increase the penalty in most cases.) The answer can be found by carefully considering the meaning of the various actions partner could take. If he doubled 6 ♠ but not 5 ♣, you would be asked to lead dummy's first-bid side suit, hearts. A double of the 5 ♣ cue-bid, but not of 6 ♠, would clearly request a club lead, as we have already seen. Thus, partner's action in doubling both 5 ♣ and 6 ♠ must be to call your attention to the one suit that he could not request by any of these other methods —diamonds. Partner has no reason to expect you to lead diamonds without the double, for declarer's 4 ◇ cue-bid may well talk you out of leading the suit if you hold a tenace such as K J 10 7 4 3.

DOUBLES OF STRONGLY BID SUIT GAMES

If the opponents bid to game with no apparent reluctance and partner suddenly doubles, he is asking for an unusual lead just as against a slam contract. For example:

(a)	SOUTH	WEST (you)	NORTH	EAST
	1 ♠	Pass	3 ♠	Pass
	4 ♠	Pass	Pass	Double
	Pass	Pass	Pass	

(b)	SOUTH	WEST (you)	NORTH	EAST
	1 ♣	Pass	1 ◊	Pass
	1 ♡	Pass	2 ♡	Pass
	2 NT	Pass	3 ♡	Pass
	4 ♡	Pass	Pass	Double
	Pass	Pass	Pass	

On auction (a), the opponents have had no trouble reaching game and may have extra strength as well. Partner's double should be treated as a Lightner double.

On auction (b), the opponents have struggled into game, and partner may be doubling to increase the penalty. He is likely to have strength in dummy's first-bid suit, diamonds, and think that the hand will go badly for declarer because the cards are lying poorly, so a diamond lead is reasonable. An unusual lead, however, is not mandatory.

Review Quiz

In each of the problems below, the auction proceeds as shown. What is your opening lead?*

* Problems 1, 3, and 10 originally appeared in *The Bridge World*.

(1)	NORTH	EAST	SOUTH	WEST
	—	—	1 ♠	3 ◊
	3 ♡	Pass	3 ♠	Pass
	4 ◊	Double	5 ♣	Pass
	6 ♠	Pass	Pass	Pass

You (West) hold:

♠ 4   ♡ 10 9   ◊ K J 10 8 7 6 2   ♣ 10 9 8

(2)	NORTH	EAST	SOUTH	WEST
	—	1 ♡	Double	2 ◊
	2 ♡	Pass	3 ♠	Pass
	4 NT	Pass	5 ♡	Pass
	6 ♠	Double	Pass	Pass
	Pass			

You (West) hold:

♠ 6 2   ♡ 10   ◊ K J 10 9 7 4 2   ♣ 8 7 4

(3)	NORTH	EAST	SOUTH	WEST
	—	—	1 ♣	1 ♠
	2 ◊	2 ♡	2 NT	Pass
	3 NT	Double	Pass	Pass
	Pass			

You (West) hold:

♠ A Q 8 5 3   ♡ 7 2   ◊ 8 5   ♣ K 8 5 3

(4)	NORTH	EAST	SOUTH	WEST
	—	—	1 ♠	Pass
	3 ♡	Pass	4 ♠	Pass
	4 NT	Pass	5 ◊	Pass
	5 NT	Pass	7 ♠	Pass
	Pass	Pass		

You (West) hold:

♠ 7 4 3   ♡ 7 6 4 2   ◊ J 6 3   ♣ Q J 10

(5)	NORTH	EAST	SOUTH	WEST
	1 ♣	1 ♡	1 NT	Pass
	3 NT	Double	Pass	Pass
	Pass			

You (West) hold:

♠ Q J 10 9   ♡ 7   ◊ 8 6 5 3   ♣ 7 4 3 2

(6)	NORTH	EAST	SOUTH	WEST
	1 ◊	Pass	2 NT	Pass
	3 NT	Double	Pass	Pass
	Pass			

You (West) hold:

♠ J 8 6 5 3   ♡ A 5   ◊ 7 6 4   ♣ 6 4 3

(7)	NORTH	EAST	SOUTH	WEST
	Pass	1 ♡	4 ♠	Pass
	Pass	Double	Pass	Pass
	Pass			

You (West) hold:

♠ 8 7 4   ♡ 8 5   ◊ 9 8 6 3 2   ♣ 10 7 4

(8)	NORTH	EAST	SOUTH	WEST
	1 ♣	Pass	1 ♠	Pass
	3 ♠	Pass	4 NT	Pass
	5 ♡	Pass	6 ♠	Pass
	Pass	Pass		

You (West) hold:

♠ 9 7 3   ♡ 8 6 4   ◊ 8 7 2   ♣ 9 7 4 2

(9)

	NORTH	EAST	SOUTH	WEST
	—	—	1 NT	Pass
	3 NT	Double	Pass	Pass
	Pass			

You (West) hold:

♠ J 10 9 8   ♡ 7 3   ◇ J 8 5 2   ♣ Q 6 2

(10)

	NORTH	EAST	SOUTH	WEST
	—	1 ♡	1 ♠	2 ♡
	3 ♡	Pass	4 ◇	Pass
	6 ◇	Double	Pass	Pass
	Redouble	Pass	Pass	Pass

You (West) hold:

♠ 8 7 2   ♡ 10 8 6 5 2   ◇ 7 6 2   ♣ K 2

In the following problems, the auction proceeds as shown. What is your call?

(11)

	NORTH	EAST	SOUTH	WEST
	1 NT	Pass	3 NT	?

You (West) hold:

♠ A Q J 9 3   ♡ 9 8 5   ◇ 7 3   ♣ 6 5 2

(12)

	NORTH	EAST	SOUTH	WEST
	1 ♣	Pass	1 ◇	Pass
	1 NT	Pass	3 NT	?

You (West) hold:

♠ Q 8 5 2   ♡ A 3   ◇ K J 10 6   ♣ 10 4 2

(13)

	NORTH	EAST	SOUTH	WEST
	1 ♡	Pass	2 NT	Pass
	3 ◇	Pass	3 ♡	Pass
	6 ♡	Pass	Pass	?

You (West) hold:

♠ K Q 5 2   ♡ A 7 3   ◇ —   ♣ 8 7 5 4 3 2

(14)	NORTH	EAST	SOUTH	WEST
	1 NT	Pass	3 NT	?

You (West) hold:

♠ 7 3   ♡ K Q J 10 8 6   ◇ 7 4 2   ♣ A 3

(15)	NORTH	EAST	SOUTH	WEST
	1 ◇	Pass	3 ♣	Pass
	3 ♡	Pass	4 ◇	Pass
	6 ◇	Pass	Pass	?

You (West) hold:

♠ A 7 3   ♡ 9 6 5 4   ◇ Q J 10   ♣ 8 4 3

(16)	NORTH	EAST	SOUTH	WEST
	—	—	1 ♣	Pass
	1 ♡	Pass	3 ♡	Pass
	4 NT	Pass	5 ◇	?

You (West) hold:

♠ 7 5 3   ♡ 8 6 4   ◇ A Q 6 2   ♣ 9 5 3

(17)	NORTH	EAST	SOUTH	WEST
	1 ♠	Pass	3 ♠	Pass
	4 NT	Pass	5 ♡	Pass
	6 ♠	Pass	Pass	?

You (West) hold:

♠ 8 5 3   ♡ 7 6 5 4 2   ◇ —   ♣ 9 7 6 3 2

(18)

NORTH	EAST	SOUTH	WEST
4 ♡	Pass	Pass	4 ♠
Double	5 ♣	Double	5 ♢
Pass	Pass	5 ♡	Pass
Pass	6 ♢	Pass	Pass
6 ♡	Pass	Pass	?

You (West) hold:

♠ A 10 9 8 7 6　　♡ 7 3　　♢ A K 10 6 4　　♣ —

(Neither side is vulnerable.)

(19)

NORTH	EAST	SOUTH	WEST
—	—	1 ♢	Pass
1 ♡	Pass	4 ♡	?

You (West) hold:

♠ J 6　　♡ A K 3　　♢ A Q 3　　♣ 8 7 6 4 2

(20)

NORTH	EAST	SOUTH	WEST
1 ♡	Pass	2 ♣	Pass
2 ♢	Pass	2 ♠	Pass
3 ♢	Pass	3 ♡	Pass
6 ♡	Pass	Pass	?

You (West) hold:

♠ 9 7 4 3　　♡ Q J 10　　♢ 8 4 2　　♣ A 6 5

Solutions

(1) *Jack of diamonds*　Respect partner's suggestion even though it involves leading away from a tenace. As it happens, partner can ruff the diamond lead and has a sure trump trick.

(2) *Jack of diamonds*　In the previous example, partner was able to double a diamond cue-bid, leaving no

doubt as to his wishes. Here, he can only suggest an unusual lead by doubling the final contract. The best bet in view of your diamond length is that he wishes to ruff a diamond lead.

(3) *Five of spades* When partner doubles a 3 NT contract and both he and you have bid a suit, prefer your own. You would lead the heart seven without the double in view of the weakness of your spade suit.

(4) *Two of hearts* Good bidding detectives are needed here. The unusual jump to 4 ♠ over the jump shift to 3 ♡ promises a solid spade suit, and the 5 NT Blackwood bid ensures that the opponents hold all four aces (else there would be no point in trying for a grand slam). Thus, the opponents should be able to claim thirteen cold tricks, and your only chance is to try for a ruff of dummy's long suit. Partner is in fact void in hearts, but could not make a Lightner double because the opponents would in all probability escape to 7 NT, which is cold.

(5) *Seven of hearts* Partner's double demands the lead of his suit.

(6) *Seven of diamonds* Partner is likely to appreciate the suit first bid by dummy much more than the moth-eaten spade suit.

(7) *Eight of hearts* There is nothing lead-directional about this double; partner is just showing a very fine hand.

(8) *Eight of diamonds* Partner failed to double the 5 ♡ response to Blackwood, and would have doubled the final contract if he felt strongly about a club lead. Therefore, if he has any powerful holding, it must be in diamonds.

(9) *Seven of hearts* Partner is asking you to hit his long suit, and based on your hand it is most likely to be hearts.

(10) *Eight of spades* Either partner's suit or the unbid suit would be normal. The opponents have misbid, and partner can cash the ace and king of spades—*if*

you lead the suit and don't give the opponents an opportunity to discard their spade losers.

(11)   *Pass*   A double to call for a spade lead is a poor risk, for you have no assurance at all of defeating the contract even if you get the lead you want.

(12)   *Pass*   A double would indicate your strength in dummy's first-bid suit, but you have no reason to believe that a diamond lead will set the hand.

(13)   *Double*   The perfect situation. If partner is in any doubt, the auction will resolve the issue, as the only unusual lead is diamonds (declarer's bid suit). A diamond lead is certain to defeat the contract, and if the opponents run to 6 NT the lead of the spade king will surely set that slam.

(14)   *Double*   You so strongly wish a heart lead that it is worth the risk of declarer's being able to run nine quick tricks.

(15)   *Pass*   You have no assurance of beating the hand, as someone could be void in spades. Furthermore, partner is likely to lead a spade (the unbid suit) if you pass, whereas a double would call for a club lead and declarer might be able to discard any spade losers.

(16)   *Double*   You have a very strong preference for a diamond lead. The opponents are not about to play the hand in diamonds.

(17)   *Pass*   Even if a diamond lead will beat 6 ♠, a run-out to 6 NT would probably be disastrous. Hope partner finds the winning lead.

(18)   *Seven diamonds*   A trap question. A club lead will probably beat the slam, but who knows what lead a double calls for after this messy auction? If partner guesses wrong, the opponents (who have a diamond void) will make the doubled slam. Play safe by conceding a few points in a 7 ◇ sacrifice.

(19)   *Double*   Dummy is marked with most of the missing strength for his 4 ♡ bid, and partner may never again be on lead. Thus, an opening diamond lead through dummy's king may be the only way to beat

the hand, and is worth the risk of declarer's holding a singleton diamond.

(20) *Double* Ordinarily, you would not request a club lead through dummy's bid suit just because you have the ace, as declarer would usually want to play the suit himself to set up discards. Here, however, you want to take your ace quickly, for the bidding suggests that declarer holds 6-5 distribution in the red suits, and if he has two black singletons he may discard his losing club on dummy's ace-king of spades. Change your hand to

♠ K 7 4 3   ♡ 7 6 2   ♢ 8 4 2   ♣ A 6 5

and you should not dream of doubling, because you want to set up a side-suit trick before your club ace is knocked out and because you have no reason to expect that a club lead will defeat the contract.

8

Lead–Directing and Lead–Inhibiting

Bids

♠ ♡ ◇ ♣

LEAD-DIRECTING BIDS

Hope may spring eternal in the human breast, but good defenders prefer to rely on certainties. When the right situation arises, a lead-directing double is far more effective than simply trusting to luck or trying to communicate with partner via ESP. If the opening leader is likely to need some assistance in finding the winning choice but a lead-directing double is not possible, a well-chosen suit bid may serve as a suitable substitute. For example:

NORTH	EAST (you)	SOUTH	WEST
1 ♣	1 ♡	1 ♠	2 ♡
2 ♠	?		

Both sides are vulnerable, and you hold:

♠ 7 5 3   ♡ A J 10 9 6 4   ◇ A 10 8 7   ♣ —

It is not at all unlikely that the opponents will wind up in 4 ♠, and you can guard against this eventuality if you act now. Your best chance to defeat the spade game is if partner leads a club for you to ruff. Unfortunately, partner is probably going to lead your suit, hearts. This loyalty, which would ordinarily be highly commendable, may prove disastrous on this hand. You cannot alert partner by doubling 4 ♠, since this would not be lead-directional but would simply be for penalties; but you can let him know what you want by cue-bidding 3 ♣. Partner must bid again, so you are assured of being able to return to hearts even if South passes. The complete deal:

NORTH
♠ K J 9 4
♡ 3
◇ 6 5 3
♣ A K Q 4 3

WEST
♠ 10
♡ K Q 8 2
◇ 9 4 2
♣ 10 9 7 6 5

EAST (you)
♠ 7 5 3
♡ A J 10 9 6 4
◇ A 10 8 7
♣ —

SOUTH
♠ A Q 8 6 2
♡ 7 5
◇ K Q J
♣ J 8 2

The bidding:

NORTH	EAST	SOUTH	WEST
1 ♣	1 ♡	1 ♠	2 ♡
2 ♠	3 ♣	4 ♠	Pass
Pass	Pass		

Without the club cue-bid, West's proper lead is the heart king, in order to take tricks before declarer can obtain any discards. The 3 ♣ bid directs West to the only winning lead, and he opens the club ten to indicate a preference for the return of the higher-ranking side suit, hearts. You ruff and underlead your heart ace to get a second club ruff, and cash your diamond ace to register a well-deserved set.

A somewhat more advanced application of the same principle occurs when you hold a singleton rather than a void and
have a quick trump entry and a probable source of access to
partner's hand. This theme has been discussed at some length in
The Bridge World, from which the following hand is taken.

NORTH
♠ Q 10 8 4
♡ 8
◊ A K 9 7
♣ A 7 6 4

WEST
♠ 7 2
♡ A K Q J 5 2
◊ 10 5 3
♣ K 3

EAST (you)
♠ A 5 3
♡ 10 9 7 6
◊ 4
♣ Q J 10 8 5

SOUTH
♠ K J 9 6
♡ 4 3
◊ Q J 8 6 2
♣ 9 2

The bidding:

NORTH	EAST	SOUTH	WEST
1 ◊	Pass	1 ♠	2 ♡
2 ♠	?		

East can see that his side has good prospects in hearts, but
the pesky opponents may persist in spades. Rather than commit
the hand directly to the cold heart game, East should bid 3 ◊,
setting the stage for the only winning defense against 4 ♠. Regardless of what South does now, East-West will proceed to 4 ♡.
If the opponents choose to go on to 4 ♠, the contract will be defeated, thanks to East's foresight. West leads a diamond in response to East's cue-bid; South wins and attacks trumps. East

takes his ace, leads a heart to West's ace, obtains a diamond ruff, and the defenders cannot be prevented from scoring the setting trick in clubs. With any other opening lead, 4 ♠ is laydown.

Another example:

SOUTH	WEST	NORTH	EAST (you)
1 ♡	1 ♠	3 ♡	?

Neither side is vulnerable, and you hold:

♠ 9 7 6 4 2   ♡ 8 5 3   ◇ —   ♣ 8 7 5 3 2

Your length in spades suggests that most or all of partner's high-card strength in the suit will be victimized by declarer's ruffs, and your hand is so poor that a slam by the opponents is a distinct possibility. A spade sacrifice is not unreasonable, but why concede a moderately large minus score when you may be able to collect a small plus? A diamond ruff will defeat the slam if partner has just one trick, and may even defeat 4 ♡ if partner's hand is strong. Bid 4 ◇, planning to return to spades if anyone doubles. Don't worry about being passed out in 4 ◇; the opponents will not show a profit if they let you play an undoubled contract when you are not vulnerable and they have a probable game or slam. It would be worse strategy to wait and make a Lightner double of the final heart contract, because the opponents might make their doubled contract even with a diamond lead and partner could not be as certain about which suit you want led.

Lead-directing bids can be very useful, but two potential disadvantages should be recognized. If the opponents believe that the lead suggested by your bid will be highly injurious, they may not bid as high as they originally intended. This is not necessarily bad, however, as you would rather have the opponents stop in game than make a slam because of the wrong opening lead, and your bid will cost only if partner would have found the winning lead without it. Second, your partner may misread your bid and cause a bidding catastrophe. To avoid this, make your lead-directing bids only when you deem it essential to get the lead you want and when you have a safe resting spot somewhere else in case something goes wrong.

Opening bids are sometimes influenced by lead-directional considerations. If the first two players pass and you are third to speak with

♠ 7 3   ♡ K 8   ♢ A K J 10   ♣ Q J 10 9 3

you should open 1 ♢, not only to enable you to rebid 2 ♣ but also to obtain a diamond lead if the opponents outbid you in the majors, as seems likely. Change the hand to

♠ 7   ♡ K 8   ♢ A K J 10   ♣ Q J 10 9 5 2

and a 1 ♢ opening, while unorthodox, would again be favored by some experts. Similarly, if you are in third seat with

♠ 8 6 4 3   ♡ A K Q 2   ♢ 7   ♣ Q 5 4 2

you should open 1 ♡. The textbook opening bid is 1 ♣, to provide for an easy rebid if partner bids diamonds; but with partner a passed hand there is a much greater danger that the opponents will outbid you. If your left-hand opponent becomes the declarer, you want a heart lead, not a club. These arguments do not apply when partner has *not* passed originally, however, for he is more likely to hold a strong hand and an unorthodox bid may simply impede your own auction.

In addition to the question of safety, overcalls require strong suits for reasons of lead-direction. Consider the following examples:

(a)	(b)	(c)
♠ K Q J 6 5	♠ J 8 6 5 3	♠ A K J 7
♡ K 6 3	♡ A K 8	♡ 8 6 3
♢ 8 5 2	♢ 8 6 3	♢ 7 5 4 2
♣ 10 6	♣ 9 4	♣ 8 4

Your side is not vulnerable, and your right-hand opponent opens the bidding with 1 ♣. You should overcall 1 ♠ on hand (a); your suit is strong enough to risk entering the auction and you want a spade lead if your left-hand opponent becomes the declarer.

Pass with hand (b). A spade overcall is more likely to be doubled by the opponents because your suit is so weak, and it may induce partner to make a disastrous opening lead from a holding such as K 4.

Most textbooks frown on overcalls with four-card suits and would therefore recommend a pass with hand (c), but the correct bid is 1 ♠. You very much want a spade lead; the bid deprives your left-hand opponent of two possible bids at the one-level, 1 ♢ and 1 ♡; and your suit is so strong that a penalty double is very unlikely even if partner raises with only three-card support. Note that you should have at least three of the top four honors to risk an overcall with a four-card suit, and should make this overcall only at the one-level when not vulnerable.

LEAD-INHIBITING BIDS

Declarer's side is also permitted to use the bidding to influence the opening lead. The following is a typical example:

SOUTH	NORTH
1 ♠	3 ♠
4 ♢	4 ♠
6 ♠	Pass

South holds:

♠ A K 9 8 6   ♡ A J 9   ♢ 7 4   ♣ A K 5

With 20 points opposite North's minimum of 13, South can tell that his partnership holds the minimum of 33 points needed for a small slam, but fears that the defenders can cash the first two diamond tricks. The correct procedure is to cue-bid clubs and hearts and then return to spades, thereby announcing to North that the diamond situation is critical. As we have seen, however, this announcement also provides valuable information for the defenders. Therefore, South chooses a small deception; he bids 4 ◊ as though to show control of the suit and then proceeds to slam, hoping to talk West out of a diamond lead. Of course, South may attempt a double-cross the next time and cue-bid a suit he does have stopped; West is on a guess. Usually, it is best to believe the opponents, but watch out for this "old chestnut." Even experts go wrong, as shown in the following hand from the 1961 Spring Nationals tournament:

```
                   NORTH
                   ♠ 10
                   ♡ Q 10 8
                   ◊ A K 9 6 5
                   ♣ A 5 4 3
   WEST                                EAST
   ♠ 5 3 2                             ♠ 9 7
   ♡ J 7 6 4 3                         ♡ A K 5
   ◊ 8 7 4                             ◊ Q J 10 3 2
   ♣ 10 6                             ♣ Q J 8
                   SOUTH
                   ♠ A K Q J 8 6 4
                   ♡ 9 2
                   ◊ —
                   ♣ K 9 7 2
```

The bidding:

SOUTH	WEST	NORTH	EAST
2 ♠	Pass	3 ◊	Pass
3 ♠	Pass	4 ♣	Pass
4 ♡ (!)	Pass	4 ♠	Pass
7 ♠	Pass	Pass	Pass

Eddie Kantar reported this deal in the April 1961 *Bridge World* with what must have been considerable regret, because (through no fault of his own) it cost his team a bushel of points.

Playing team-of-four, he and his partner made game in spades with the North-South cards, and in the other room the bidding went as shown above. Whether the 4 ♡ bid was lunatic or genius is by no means clear, but West was taken in and led a spade, allowing declarer to wrap up the contract.* (However, Kantar's team won the match anyway in spite of this unfriendly result.)

Another hoary trick occurs when South, holding a long and strong minor, opens with one of the other minor and then jumps to 3 NT. He reasons that the final contract will in all probability be 3 NT, so the minor-suit opening bid will not affect the North-South auction and may inhibit an effective opening lead.

A third example occurs in the following situation:

SOUTH	NORTH
1 ♡	2 ♡
?	

* Declarer wins the spade in dummy, ruffs a diamond (unnecessary as the cards lie, but essential if West has three diamonds to one or more honors) and runs off all the trumps, producing the following position with East still to discard on the last trump:

NORTH
♠ —
♡ Q
◊ A K 9
♣ A 5

WEST
Immaterial

EAST
♠ —
♡ A
◊ Q J 10
♣ Q J 8

SOUTH
♠ —
♡ 9 2
◊ —
♣ K 9 7 2

If East pitches a club, South's clubs are all good and he easily wins the rest of the tricks with four clubs and two diamonds. A red-suit discard is equally fatal; suppose East throws a diamond. South crosses to the club ace and runs three diamond tricks, pitching two hearts and a club, and on the last diamond East must unguard either hearts or clubs and give South his thirteenth trick.

South holds:

♠ 8   ♡ A Q 10 7 4   ◇ A K Q 7 2   ♣ 7 6

After North's single raise, game is very likely and slam is remote, and South should simply bid 4 ♡. There is no bonus for locating a second playable trump suit, and a diamond bid can only help the opponents find their best lead. A well-known deceptive procedure in such instances is to bid the weak suit (here, 3 ♣) on the way to game in the hope that West will be deterred from the one lead that appears most threatening to declarer. As before, South should vary his tactics and at times bid the suit in which he does in fact have strength, else West will know exactly what to do when South trots out his false bid.

Review Quiz

In each of the following problems, the auction proceeds as shown, and neither side is vulnerable. What call do you make?

(1)	NORTH	EAST	SOUTH	WEST
	—	—	1 ♣	?

You (West) hold:

♠ 7 6   ♡ A K Q 5   ◇ 8 5 4 2   ♣ Q 8 3

(2)	NORTH	EAST	SOUTH	WEST
	1 ♡	2 ◇	3 ♣	?

You (West) hold:

♠ J 9 7 6 3 2   ♡ A 6   ◇ K 10 8 3   ♣ 7

(3)	NORTH	EAST	SOUTH	WEST
(a)	—	—	—	?
(b)	—	Pass	Pass	?

You (West) hold:

♠ A K Q 7   ♡ 9 8 3   ◇ 7 4   ♣ Q 10 4 2

(4)	NORTH	EAST	SOUTH	WEST
	1 ♡	1 ♠	2 ♣	?

You (West) hold:

♠ J 3 2   ♡ J 8 4   ◇ A K 8 6 5   ♣ 8 7

(5)	NORTH	EAST	SOUTH	WEST
	1 ♠	2 ♡	6 ♠	?

You (West) hold:

♠ 8 5 3   ♡ K J 8 5 2   ◇ K Q 9 7 6   ♣ —

(6)	NORTH	EAST	SOUTH	WEST
	—	—	1 ◇	?

You (West) hold:

♠ A K J 8   ♡ 6 5 4 2   ◇ 8   ♣ K 10 8 4

In each of the following problems, the auction and vulnerability are as shown. You are West. What is your opening lead?

(7)	NORTH	EAST	SOUTH	WEST
	—	—	1 ♡	2 ◇
	3 ♡	4 ♣	Double	Pass
	Pass	4 ◇	4 ♡	Pass
	Pass	5 ◇	5 ♡	Pass
	Pass	Pass		

You (West) hold:

♠ A 5   ♡ 7   ◇ K Q J 9 6 3   ♣ 9 7 5 3

(North-South vulnerable)

(8)	NORTH	EAST	SOUTH	WEST
	—	1 ♠	2 ♡	Pass
	3 ♡	4 ◇	4 ♡	Pass
	Pass	Pass		

You (West) hold:

♠ 8 3   ♡ J 8 5   ◇ J 6 5   ♣ 7 6 4 3 2

(Neither side vulnerable)

(9)	NORTH	EAST	SOUTH	WEST
	1 ♣	1 ♡	1 ♠	Pass
	3 ♠	Pass	4 ♠	Pass
	Pass	Pass		

You (West) hold:

♠ K 8 7   ♡ 8 6 3   ◇ Q J 10 9   ♣ 7 4 2

(Neither side vulnerable)

(10)	NORTH	EAST	SOUTH	WEST
	—	1 ♠	2 ♡	2 ♠
	3 ♡	4 ◇	4 ♡	Pass
	Pass	4 ♠	5 ♡	Double
	Pass	Pass	Pass	

You (West) hold:

♠ 10 7 6 3   ♡ 8 4   ◇ 7 6 3   ♣ A Q 10 3

(East-West vulnerable)

Solutions

(1)   *One heart*   All sorts of good things may happen. You may get a crucial heart lead against the enemy's contract; the opponents may eschew 3 NT for fear of five fast heart losers; an opponent with length in hearts may expect his partner to be short and over-bid; or you may buy the contract. Even though you have only four hearts, you are relatively safe because of your great strength.

(2)   *Four clubs*   You want a club lead against a heart contract so that you can later win the trump ace, cross to partner's probable diamond ace, and secure a club ruff, and you should have a safe spot in 4 ♢. If South becomes declarer at a club contract, you haven't lost anything.

(3)   (a)   *Pass*   You are not strong enough to open the bidding in first seat.
       (b)   *One spade*   With partner a passed hand, the opponents are likely to buy the contract. Direct the lead while you can. You plan to pass anything partner bids.

(4)   *Two diamonds*   If the opponents were not a factor, you would raise to 2 ♠, but you want a diamond lead against a heart contract. You might be able to give partner a quick diamond ruff, or lead through a spade honor in declarer's hand.

(5)   *Seven clubs*   You will return to 7 ♡ if doubled. Do *not* double 7 ♠ if the opponents bid it, for that would ask for an unusual lead (presumably not hearts or clubs, the suits bid by your side); be content to get your club ruff and defeat the grand slam one trick undoubled.

(6)   *Double*   This is the wrong type of hand for a 1 ♠ overcall, because the hand may well belong to you in a heart or club contract.

(7)   *Nine of clubs*   Apparently, East's 4 ♣ bid is lead-directional and South is unaware of what is going on. Lead the nine because you have a sure entry in the higher-ranking side suit, spades. As it happens, partner has the singleton ace of clubs and a club lead, spade return, and club ruff is the only way to defeat the contract.

(8)   *Eight of spades*   Partner's 4 ◇ bid simply shows a very powerful hand and a good second suit and does not command a diamond lead. You may be able to score a ruff or overruff on the third round of spades.

(9)   *Eight of hearts*   Trust partner's overcalls unless previous experience dictates to the contrary.

(10)   *Four of hearts*   Partner's 4 ◇ bid could be lead-directional, but in all likelihood he is just showing you where his strength is to enable you to make a sensible decision over the probable 5 ♡ sacrifice. With your side marked with strength in all suits, discards are not imminent and you should lead a trump to cut down the opponents' ruffing power as the best way of inflicting the maximum penalty.

9

Lead Expertise

♠   ♡   ◇   ♣

A careful study and application of the principles in the preceding chapters will render your opening leads considerably above average. However, you will be even more effective if you make judicious use of certain expert techniques in the appropriate situations. Many writers avoid these topics for fear that they are too complex for the typical reader; but anyone perspicacious enough to invest in a book devoted solely to opening leads is clearly a cut above average and should find considerable interest in topics somewhat out of the ordinary. Therefore, let's look at some intriguing ways of bringing perdition down upon the head of the unfortunate declarer.

FALSE-CARDING ON LEAD

Standard leads, such as the fourth-best card or queen from Q J 10, have the important advantage of advising partner as to your holding in the suit. Declarer may also profit from this knowledge, but you should be willing to risk paying this price most of the time. After all, declarer can see both his hand and the dummy, while the defenders are more in the dark about the best methods of defense. Therefore, the information provided by your lead is usually more helpful to partner than to declarer.

Suppose, however, that you have so much high-card strength that partner is almost surely broke. Now the lead of an unusual card may deceive declarer and do little harm to partner, who is likely to be taking only a remote interest in the proceedings. Also, if declarer is an intense sort of fellow who carefully watches every card and partner tends to ignore what is going on, a deceptive lead may have everything to gain and nothing to lose; partner can't be misled by what he doesn't notice.

NORTH	EAST	SOUTH	WEST (you)
1 ◇	Pass	2 ♣	Pass
2 ◇	Pass	3 NT	Pass
Pass	Pass		

Your side is vulnerable, and you (West) hold:

♠ A K 8 5 2   ♡ 7 6   ◇ K 5 3   ♣ A 5 2

Your best chance to defeat the contract is to lead a spade, find the suit split 3-3 in the North-South hands, and gain reentry with the club ace to run four spade tricks. Declarer may decide to attack diamonds instead of clubs, however, and is likely to be very pleased at the location of your king. He may even be able to run nine tricks without the aid of the club suit. Can anything be done about this? Declarers are prone to worry a great deal about such things as running suits, and the lead of the *deuce* of spades may lull him into a sense of false security. You don't care if partner is misled, for he undoubtedly has no entry and will not play an important role in the defense. The deceptive lead is in fact essential, for the complete deal is as follows:

NORTH
♠ 9 7 4
♡ A Q 3
♢ A Q J 9 6
♣ 8 3

WEST
♠ A K 8 5 2
♡ 7 6
♢ K 5 3
♣ A 5 2

EAST
♠ 6 3
♡ 9 8 5 4 2
♢ 8 4 2
♣ 9 6 4

SOUTH
♠ Q J 10
♡ K J 10
♢ 10 7
♣ K Q J 10 7

If you lead the spade five, declarer will observe that the deuce is missing and reason that you probably have a five-card suit. Therefore, he cannot afford to knock out the club ace, as you will run enough tricks to defeat the contract. He must instead fall back on the diamond finesse, which will give him nine tricks and his contract.

If you lead the two of spades, however, declarer will reason that you have only four cards in the suit. It would therefore be foolish to risk the diamond finesse, which would give your side five tricks if it lost (three spades, one diamond, and the club ace). South will consequently play clubs, secure in the "knowledge" that the defenders can cash at most three spade tricks and one diamond. However, he will be in for a surprise!

The reverse of the above false-carding situation occurs when you want to persuade declarer that he is in danger when in fact all is well. Suppose that the bidding is the same as in the above example, and you hold:

♠ A K 5 2   ♡ 7 6 3   ♢ A 5 2   ♣ K 5 3

With partner marked with a virtual Yarborough, your chances of defeating the contract aren't very good. You need a 3-3-3 division of the remaining spades to enable you to take three spade tricks, and must also score the king of clubs as well as your diamond ace. Fortunately, your club king is behind declarer's bid suit, but can he be induced to take the finesse? Lead the *five* of spades! The complete deal:

NORTH
♠ 9 7 4
♡ A Q J
◇ K Q J 8 6
♣ 8 2

WEST
♠ A K 5 2
♡ 7 6 3
◇ A 5 2
♣ K 5 3

EAST
♠ 8 6 3
♡ 8 5 4 2
◇ 9 4 3
♣ 9 6 4

SOUTH
♠ Q J 10
♡ K 10 9
◇ 10 7
♣ A Q J 10 7

The lead of the spade five is likely to induce declarer to think that you have a five-card suit and that he cannot afford to lose the lead. He will therefore take the club finesse, presenting you with the vital fifth trick. With the pedestrian lead of the spade deuce, it will be much easier for declarer to read the situation and find the winning procedure of developing the diamond suit.

At times, it will also be necessary for you to deceive declarer as to your suit length in a suit contract. A remarkable example of this occurs in the following deal:

SOUTH	WEST (you)	NORTH	EAST
1 ♠	Pass	2 ◇	Pass
3 ♠	Pass	4 ♣	Pass
4 ◇	Pass	5 ♠	Pass
5 NT	Pass	6 ♠	Pass
Pass	Pass		

South's 5 NT bid is the Grand Slam Force, inquiring as to the strength of North's spade holding, and the 6 ♠ bid shows one of the top three spade honors. (Remember, you are entitled to know the meaning of any artificial bids used by the opponents before you lead.) Your hand is:

♠ Q J 8 7   ♡ J 6 3   ◇ 4 2   ♣ 8 7 6 4

You have two potential trump tricks, but declarer may be able to foil you by one of two methods. The bidding suggests that South has no losers in the side suits (since he was apparently willing to contract for a grand slam if North's trumps were strong enough) and that the spade suit is distributed approximately as follows:

NORTH
♠ A 10 4

WEST (you)   EAST
♠ Q J 8 7   ♠ —

SOUTH
♠ K 9 6 5 3 2

The standard safety play in such situations is to lead a low spade to dummy's ten. This may cost an unnecessary trick, but insures declarer against the loss of two trump tricks and saves the slam as the cards lie. The second danger is that declarer may guess your side-suit distribution, eliminate your cards in the non-trump suits, and then endplay you in spades. The best way of guarding against both possibilities is to lead the diamond deuce. If declarer believes this to be a singleton, he will not take the spade safety play for fear of East's winning the first spade trick and giving you a diamond ruff. Also, the lead of a low card from a doubleton is almost certain to cause him to miscount your hand and allow you to overruff before the endplay arises. The threat of the endplay is in fact the main danger, for the complete deal is:

```
                          NORTH
                          ♠ A 4 2
                          ♡ Q 5
                          ◇ K Q 7 5
                          ♣ K Q 5 3

          WEST                              EAST
          ♠ Q J 8 7                         ♠ —
          ♡ J 6 3                           ♡ 10 9 7 4 2
          ◇ 4 2                             ◇ J 10 8 6 3
          ♣ 8 7 6 4                         ♣ J 10 9

                          SOUTH
                          ♠ K 10 9 6 5 3
                          ♡ A K 8
                          ◇ A 9
                          ♣ A 2
```

Declarer can make his slam as follows: He wins the opening diamond lead with the ace and plays a spade to dummy's ace, looking pained when East shows out. He now plays the ace and king of clubs and ruffs a club, enters dummy with a diamond and ruffs another club, and plays the queen, king and ace of hearts. You have been compelled to follow suit during this process, and are now reduced to your three remaining trumps. South plays the spade nine; you win but are endplayed and must concede the last two tricks and the slam.

If declarer tries to shorten his trump holding by ruffing diamonds instead of clubs, or by attempting to ruff each minor suit once (his best percentage play), you will overruff the third round of diamonds and exit in a side suit, and the slam will be defeated. Declarer has no way of knowing which minor suit to ruff, but will get a useful clue during the play when East follows with the

three top clubs on the first three rounds of the suit. The lead of
the diamond deuce, however, is likely to lead him astray by sug-
gesting that you hold length in the suit, and he may assume that
East is false-carding with ♣ J 10 9 8.*

In rare instances, partner may know the length of declarer's
suit for a certainty without any help from you. In such occasions, your lead should be designed to withhold information from
declarer. For example:

SOUTH	WEST (you)	NORTH	EAST
1 NT	Pass	2 ♣	Pass
2 ♡	Pass	3 NT	Pass
Pass	Pass		

North's 2 ♣ response is the Stayman convention. The majority of players do not open 1 NT with a five-card (or longer)
major suit, so South should have exactly four hearts, and partner
can figure this out regardless of your lead. Thus, holding

♠ J 8 6   ♡ A Q J 5 3   ◇ 8 5   ♣ K 6 5

you might just as well lead the three of hearts.

Deception on opening lead can be designed to conceal your
strength as well as your distribution. The following is a common
yet very effective example:

SOUTH	WEST (you)	NORTH	EAST
—	—	1 ♣	Pass
1 NT	Pass	Pass	Pass
		(or 2 NT,	
		or 3 NT)	

---

* Note that declarer can also make 6 NT if he guesses West's distribution, which would justify the lead of the diamond deuce against that
contract as well. The winning line (assuming a club lead) is for South
to win the club ace and lead a spade to the ace. Upon discovering the bad
split, declarer now cashes the queen, king, and ace of hearts, pitching a
low diamond from dummy, and wins the king and queen of diamonds,
discarding a low spade from his hand. West cannot discard a club without establishing North's long club as the twelfth trick, so he pitches a
spade, whereupon declarer ducks a spade completely and claims the
remainder.

You hold:

♠ 8 3   ♥ 7 4 2   ♦ K 9 5   ♣ A Q J 10 8

Lead the queen of clubs! Dummy is likely to have the king, and you will do well to look like a man without the ace if the suit is distributed as follows:

DUMMY
♣ K 7 6 3

YOU   PARTNER
♣ A Q J 10 8   ♣ 9 5

DECLARER
♣ 4 2

When you lead the queen, declarer should play low from dummy, and he should also duck when you continue with the jack. (To see why, exchange the nine and ace of clubs in the defenders' hands.) When you now lead the club ten, declarer will probably go wrong and duck again, playing East for ♣ A 9 5. Even if he guesses right, you haven't lost anything.

Another common but nevertheless useful false-card is the following:

NORTH
♠ Q J 10 3 2

WEST   EAST
♠ A K 8 5   ♠ 9 6 4

SOUTH
♠ 7

South is playing a 6 ♥ contract, and North has bid spades. West will defeat the contract if he can score two spade tricks, but he knows that South is likely to have a singleton. He therefore leads the spade ace (concealing the king) and shifts suits, hoping to induce South to take the ruffing finesse in spades instead of an alternate line of play that will be successful.

The complete deal:

NORTH
♠ Q J 10 3 2
♡ J 10 9
◇ A Q 7
♣ Q J

WEST
♠ A K 8 5
♡ 3
◇ K 9 5 3
♣ 10 8 6 4

EAST
♠ 9 6 4
♡ 4 2
◇ 6 4 2
♣ 9 7 5 3 2

SOUTH
♠ 7
♡ A K Q 8 7 6 5
◇ J 10 8
♣ A K

The bidding:

SOUTH	WEST	NORTH	EAST
2 ♡	Pass	2 ♠	Pass
3 ♡	Pass	4 ♡	Pass
5 ♣	Pass	5 ◇	Pass
6 ♡	Pass	Pass	Pass

The slam is made easily if South takes the diamond finesse. If West leads the spade ace and shifts to the nine of diamonds, declarer may be persuaded that East holds the spade king and see no reason to risk the diamond finesse. If he does go up with the diamond ace and rely on the ruffing finesse, the result will be most gratifying to the defenders.

One principle that helps declarers plan the play is that high-card strength tends to be evenly divided between opponents who have not bid. This consideration may affect your lead in some instances. If, for example, you are on lead against a 4 ♠ contract with

♠ 8 6   ♡ 7 3 2   ◇ A K Q J 10   ♣ 9 4 2

and have decided to lead a diamond, you probably should lead the queen and follow with the jack. Partner will hardly be misled once you win the first two tricks or declarer ruffs in, and if declarer thinks your partner has the ace and king of diamonds he is more likely to play you for any other missing honors, such as the queen of trumps. If you proudly announce possession of the ace, king, and queen of diamonds on the first three leads of the suit, a good declarer will resolve any guesses in favor of finessing through partner—and you can tell from your hand that he'll be right. Conversely, if you hold

♠ Q 8 6   ♡ 7 3   ◇ A K Q J 10   ♣ 9 4 2

you should lead the king, ace, and queen of diamonds, because you want declarer to play partner for the spade queen.

One false-card to avoid is the lead of the jack of trumps from queen-jack doubleton. This is very well known, and the lead of the jack of trumps is so peculiar that declarer will probably figure out what is going on. Besides, you are likely to score a trick against a good declarer if you leave well enough alone.

False-carding on opening lead can be very effective when the right situation arises, but you should handle this weapon with care. Remember, you run the great risk of misleading partner as well as declarer, which may be fatal to the defense. When in doubt, make your natural lead, and you will be less likely to encounter one of the most fearsome wild beasts known to mankind—an angry partner.

UNUSUAL HIGH-CARD LEADS

Unless you hold a sequence, it is usually inadvisable to lead an honor card. There are, however, some important exceptions to this useful rule. One of these was discussed in Chapter 5, where the lead of an unsupported honor in partner's suit was shown to be highly effective when you wished to remain on lead. A second exception occurs when declarer is playing a notrump contract and is likely to have a singleton in dummy's suit:

SOUTH	WEST (you)	NORTH	EAST
1 ♣	Pass	1 ◇	Pass
1 ♠	Pass	3 ♣	Pass
3 NT	Pass	Pass	Pass

You (West) hold:

♠ Q 7 4 3   ♡ A 7 5 3   ◇ K 5 4   ♣ Q 6

South has bid clubs and spades and is likely to be well off in hearts for his notrump bid. Ordinarily, the lead of the unbid suit would be reasonable, but you don't have enough length or strength to prove troublesome to declarer. A heart might be right, but a diamond through dummy's suit is a better shot, and the correct lead is the king in case South has a singleton honor. Admittedly, it takes some intestinal fortitude to make this lead, but in fact it is not at all uncommon among experts (though it rarely seems to find its way into bridge books). Be sure, however, that all the signs are right: dummy has bid the suit or is marked with a four-card holding, declarer is marked with shortness in the suit (probably a singleton), your own holding is fairly short so that you have a good chance of finding length in partner's hand, and no other lead is particularly attractive.

Under certain conditions, it is correct to lead the high card from very long suits against notrump contracts. If you are going to lead from K J 10 9 4 3 and have some side entries, you might as well lead the king in case the queen is singleton. Catching a singleton ace won't help unless the queen is guarded no more than once, which is highly improbable. Similarly, lead the queen from Q 10 9 8 5 3. Also, if you hold a strong hand and suspect that partner is broke, you should lead the ace from A Q 10 6 4 3 against a notrump contract. Once you see the dummy, you can decide whether to continue with the queen (necessary if the jack is doubleton to avoid giving declarer two stoppers) or a small one (essential if the king is doubleton). Since partner is unlikely to ever gain the lead, you will have to do all the attacking yourself, and it is better to make your plans after you see the dummy.* If, however, your hand is not overly strong and partner is likely to hold an entry, make your normal lead of the fourth-best card. Similar reasoning applies when holding A J 10 8 4 3.

UNDERLEADING ACES AGAINST SUIT CONTRACTS

Very bad things can happen to a defender presumptuous enough to underlead an ace against a suit contract. He may lose his ace later on to declarer's ruffing power and never get the trick he deserves, or partner may be misled and make an abysmal error. When such boldness is well timed, however, it may be amply rewarded. Here's an example from the June 1963 *Bridge World:*

SOUTH	WEST (you)	NORTH	EAST
1 ♣	1 ♡	2 ◊	4 ♡
Pass	Pass	5 ♣	Pass
Pass	Pass		

You (West) hold:

   ♠ A Q 9   ♡ A Q 10 4 2   ◊ 8 6 5 3   ♣ 10

---

* Don't worry about the convention that asks partner to drop his highest card on the ace. Since you're sure that he is broke, his play to the first trick is undoubtedly immaterial.

Partner's triple raise in all probability shows five-card support, so you cannot expect more than one heart trick to survive before declarer starts making a thorough nuisance of himself by ruffing. Your diamond holding suggests that declarer will have ample discards once he gains the lead, so you cannot wait to collect two spade tricks. Speed is essential, and you should gamble on finding your partner with the heart king for his bid so that you can get a fast spade lead through declarer's probable king. Lead a low heart! The full hand:

NORTH
♠ 7 4
♡ 7
◇ A K J 9 7 4
♣ Q J 7 6

WEST
♠ A Q 9
♡ A Q 10 4 2
◇ 8 6 5 3
♣ 10

EAST
♠ 8 6 5 3 2
♡ K J 9 5 3
◇ 10
♣ 9 4

SOUTH
♠ K J 10
♡ 8 6
◇ Q 2
♣ A K 8 5 3 2

With any defense except a low heart lead and spade shift, South wraps up his contract.*

COMMUNICATIONS-ATTACKING LEADS

Oddly enough, declarer may sometimes come to grief if forced to play his best suit before he is ready. For example:

---

* A suit-preference lead by West is not essential; it should be quite obvious to East what shift is desired.

NORTH
♠ 4 2
♡ 9 5 3
♦ K Q J 10 8 7
♣ 10 7

WEST   EAST
♠ A 8   ♠ 7 6 3
♡ Q 10 8 6   ♡ K J 2
♦ 9 5   ♦ 6 4 2
♣ K J 9 4 2   ♣ Q 8 6 3

SOUTH
♠ K Q J 10 9 5
♡ A 7 4
♦ A 3
♣ A 5

The bidding:

NORTH	EAST	SOUTH	WEST
3 ♦	Pass	4 ♠	Pass
Pass	Pass		

North's preempt shows a long and strong suit without much strength on the side, and West will do very well if he leads a diamond. South wins with the ace and leads a trump, and West goes right up with the ace and plays a second diamond. Declarer is now in a fine fix: If he continues drawing trumps, he will never be able to get back to dummy's good diamonds and will lose one spade, two hearts, and one club. If he leads a diamond, West will ruff. Regardless of what declarer does now, West's imaginative defense defeats the contract. The diamond lead does risk allowing declarer to take some quick pitches on dummy's suit if he has a singleton or void, but West's diamond shortness and ace of trumps entry provide a margin of safety.

TOURNAMENT TIPS

Most of the principles discussed in this book are fully applicable to tournament play, but some exceptions should be noted. Let's consider the various forms of scoring separately.

IMP and Total-Point Team-of-Four: This form of play is much like rubber bridge, and your primary objective is to defeat the contract and not be overly concerned about yielding an overtrick or two. Therefore, no changes are recommended.

Board-a-match Team-of-Four: This is an entirely different game. For each hand, you score one point if you beat the other team, one-half point if you tie them, and no points if they defeat you, and the size of the victory or defeat is irrelevant. It costs just as much to drop an overtrick on defense while your teammates in the other room are held to their contract as it does to suffer a 1,700-point penalty while your teammates are making a part-score.

If you believe your team to be superior to the opponents, you should tend to be conservative on opening lead. You have less information at your disposal when on opening lead than at any other time during the defense, and a bad lead may put to ruin all the expertise of your teammate who is the declarer in the other room. Of course, you should still take advantage of the various clues at your disposal and act when they point strongly towards a particular action, but when matters are uncertain play safe, try and duplicate the lead that will be made in the other room, and look to win the board by other means. For example, lead the king from K Q J 3 2 or A K J 7 5 or the jack from J 10 9 6 3 against a notrump contract even if the suit is bid on your right.

If, on the other hand, your opponents are more experienced, you can afford to take some chances. You have less to lose, for the enemy declarer is likely to outplay his counterpart on your team. However, maintain your self-discipline and make the standard lead when it is indicated. (For all you know, the expert in the other room may try something fancy and commit an egregious blunder.)

Match-pointed pairs: This event is scored like a board-a-match team of four except that your score is compared to a large number of pairs playing the same cards, so that your award on any one hand may range from zero to 12 (or more) depending on how many pairs you beat. You can no longer afford the luxury of assuming that you can defeat every contract, for it can cost just as much to let the opponents make an overtrick as it will to incur a 2,000-point set. If your pair is the only one in the room that allows the opponents to make 5 ♠ and every other declarer is held to four, you will get no points at all on that hand (for everyone else will have done better). Conversely, if you are the only ones to hold your opponents to 4 ♠ and every other declarer makes 5 ♠ (or more), you will receive a top score. At match-points, therefore, you should not make a lead that is likely to give declarer an undeserved overtrick or two just because it has a long-shot chance of defeating the contract (though such a strategy would be proper at rubber bridge).* There are a few occasions when you should go all-out to defeat the contract (for example, if the opponents are in an unusual contract which no one else in the field is likely to bid), but you should usually avoid desperation shots unless you need a good score or unless all indications point to the unusual lead. Of course, if you have several good clues at your disposal, that is another matter entirely. Now you stand to get a good score, for most players are not familiar with more than the most straightforward procedures and you are likely to profit from your superior skill.

Look to run suits against notrump contracts more often at match-points. Experienced tournament players will be willing to

---

* By all means, however, give declarer one undeserved trick if you will get two tricks back. A partner of mine once held ♠ 3 ♡ 9 8 4 2 ◇ 6 4 2 ♣ A Q J 8 2 and, against the auction 2 NT—3 NT, led the club queen. Declarer happily won his doubleton king and ran off nine tricks, making exactly 3 NT. This was a bad score—for *declarer*. At the other tables, the opening leader was afraid to tackle clubs after declarer's strong opening and declarer never got a trick with his club king, but he had time to safely take *two* finesses through me (one a most unlikely double finesse against the queen-jack of spades) and make *four* notrump.

risk somewhat shaky notrump contracts, for they will reap substantial dividends if they score a mere 10 points more than the
other players. Also, you can be more free with your lead-directing
overcalls at match-points, for a large set will simply represent one
bad score rather than a huge numerical deficit that will take the
whole evening to erase. Furthermore, just cashing out your tricks
may bring you a fine score, for many other pairs may go to sleep
with an ace or two. Holding A K J 5 3, lead the king against the
auction 1 NT–3 NT even with no outside entries and consider
cashing the ace if dummy comes down with a powerhouse. If all
the other declarers are making 3 NT with three overtricks, you
will get just as many points for holding the player at your table to
5 NT as you would for defeating the contract—a cold top.

A similar example occurs in the following situation:

WEST (you)	NORTH	EAST	SOUTH
1 ♠	2 ♣	Pass	2 NT
Pass	3 NT	Pass	Pass
Pass			

You (West) hold:

♠ 10 8 7 5 4   ♡ A Q 10 3   ◇ Q J 2   ♣ A

You can tell that partner is almost surely broke, and that the
opponents are well prepared for a spade lead. You cannot afford
to play passively, for you will find it very difficult to discard safely
when North's clubs are run. The expert lead is the ace of hearts,
attempting to develop a trick or two before the ace of clubs is
driven out. The heart ace is selected so that you can see the
dummy before deciding how to proceed; you will want to continue with a low heart if dummy has a doubleton king, but should
play the queen of hearts if dummy has a doubleton jack. This
hand is from actual play, and dummy held the doubleton king-
jack of hearts. Leading either the ace or a low heart held declarer
to nine tricks for a superb match-point score; most Souths easily
made *five* notrump after the pedestrian spade lead.

Review Quiz

Although short, this quiz is quite difficult, and you will be doing very well if you get three or more correct. In each case, the auction proceeds as shown; what is your opening lead?

(1)

NORTH	EAST	SOUTH	WEST
—	—	1 ♢	Pass
1 ♠	Pass	3 NT	Pass
Pass	Pass		

You (West) hold:

♠ K 5 2   ♡ 9 8 7   ♢ 5 3   ♣ A Q 10 7 6

(2)

NORTH	EAST	SOUTH	WEST
—	—	1 NT	Pass
3 NT	Pass	Pass	Pass

You (West) hold:

♠ Q 8 7   ♡ K J 7 4 2   ♢ A Q 7   ♣ K 4

(3)

NORTH	EAST	SOUTH	WEST
1 ♢	Pass	2 ♣	Pass
2 ♢	Pass	3 ♢	Pass
3 ♠	Pass	3 NT	Pass
Pass	Pass		

You (West) hold:

♠ A Q 3   ♡ A 7 5 2   ♢ K 5 3   ♣ 10 6 4

(4)

NORTH	EAST	SOUTH	WEST
1 ♣	Pass	2 NT	Pass
3 NT	Pass	Pass	Pass

You (West) hold:

♠ K 3   ♡ 7 4   ◇ A Q 10 8 6 5   ♣ A 7 4

(5)

	NORTH	EAST	SOUTH	WEST
	1 ♠	4 ◇	4 ♡	5 ◇
	5 ♡	Pass	Pass	Pass

You (West) hold:

♠ 9 7 5 4 3   ♡ 6   ◇ A 8   ♣ A Q 6 4 2

(Both sides are vulnerable.)

Solutions

(1) *King of spades*   This may cost an overtrick or two, but gives you the best chance of defeating the contract. You may smother a singleton spade honor in declarer's hand and run the whole suit, or find an entry to partner's hand for a lead through declarer's probable club king. The reason for avoiding the standard lead of the club seven is that the 3 NT rebid is often based on a long and strong minor suit, and declarer is likely to be able to run nine tricks once he obtains the lead. A typical South hand would be

♠ J   ♡ A J 3   ◇ A K Q 10 8 6 4   ♣ K 3

(2) *Two of hearts*   Partner is sure to have a Yarborough as there are only 25 high-card points missing, so you may as well try and mislead declarer. Perhaps he will do something silly if he thinks you have only four hearts. The heart seven might also work by persuading declarer that your lead is "top of nothing."

(3) *Queen of spades*   South is marked with a heart stopper for his 3 NT bid, and your heart holding is very unexciting. A first-rate deceptive lead is available in the

spade suit. North is marked with the spade king for his
3 ♠ bid, which surely was intended to show a spade
stopper and invite 3 NT. If declarer has the ten and partner the jack, you are in business. Declarer will duck the
opening lead in dummy (the correct play; he does not
want East to win the ace and lead through his ten) and
you will continue with a small one, and declarer will play
you for Q J 3 and duck again. Partner will win and shift
to a heart through declarer's king.

(4)   *Ace of diamonds*   You have so much strength that
partner is marked with a bust, so any diamond leads will
have to come from you. You will judge whether to follow
with the diamond queen or a small diamond after you see
the dummy.

(5)   *Eight of diamonds*   The best way to justify this lead is
to present the complete deal, taken from the September
1964 *Bridge World:*

NORTH
♠ A K J 10 8
♡ A 10 8 5
◇ 5
♣ 10 9 3

WEST   EAST
♠ 9 7 5 4 3   ♠ 6
♡ 6   ♡ 4
◇ A 8   ◇ K Q J 10 9 7 4 3
♣ A Q 6 4 2   ♣ 8 7 5

SOUTH
♠ Q 2
♡ K Q J 9 7 3 2
◇ 6 2
♣ K J

The low diamond lead and club return by East is the only
defense to defeat the contract.

10

An Opening Lead Hall of Fame

♠ ♡ ◇ ♣

Opening leads are frequently called the most difficult part of bridge, and great opening leads are therefore worthy of special mention. When a defender rises to the challenge and makes a spectacular lead in actual play, his achievement deserves to be recorded for posterity. Success, however, cannot be the sole criterion for issuing awards of excellence, for it is quite possible to construct hands on which even the most absurd-looking leads happen to be correct. For example, consider the following hand from an article of mine in the March 1965 *Bridge Journal:*

```
                    NORTH
                    ♠ A K 3 2
                    ♡ A K Q 2
                    ◇ —
                    ♣ A K Q J 10
   WEST                             EAST
   ♠ J 10 9 8                       ♠ 5 4
   ♡ J 10 9 8                       ♡ 4 3
   ◇ J 7 6 5                        ◇ K Q 10
   ♣ 8                              ♣ 9 6 5 4 3 2
                    SOUTH
                    ♠ Q 7 6
                    ♡ 7 6 5
                    ◇ A 9 8 4 3 2
                    ♣ 7
```

South is the declarer in 7 NT, and will easily fulfill his contract if West makes the normal lead from one of his major-suit sequences. The first trick is won in dummy and declarer runs the club suit, West discarding four diamonds. South then enters his hand with the spade queen and lays down the diamond ace. West is squeezed and must unguard one of the major suits, whereupon dummy discards in the other major and declarer easily takes the rest of the tricks.

The final result will be quite different if West makes the strange lead of a diamond away from his jack. This egregious lead squeezes dummy before declarer can get his own squeeze going, and the grand slam is defeated. I called this play the "nightmare squeeze," partly because it seems like something out of a bad dream to the unfortunate declarer and partly because the hand took place only in my imagination. Here's another artificial example:

NORTH
♠ J 10
♡ 5
♢ 8 6 5 4 3
♣ 9 7 6 5 2

WEST
♠ Q 9 6
♡ K J 9 7
♢ 9 2
♣ Q J 10 4

EAST
♠ 4 2
♡ Q 10 6 4 3
♢ Q J 10 7
♣ 8 3

SOUTH
♠ A K 8 7 5 3
♡ A 8 2
♢ A K
♣ A K

South plays 6 ♠, and easily makes his slam after the lead of a heart, diamond or club by simply ruffing two hearts in dummy. If West leads a low trump, South can ruff only one heart, but he no longer has to lose a spade trick and still makes his small slam. The double-dummy lead of the spade queen, however, wrecks the contract. If South ruffs a heart with dummy's last trump, he will lose one heart and one spade; and if declarer draws trumps, he will lose two heart tricks.

As in the above two examples, any weird lead that a defender happens to throw out on the table may strike oil if the rest of the cards are distributed in a particular way, but this does not necessarily constitute a recommendation for the sagacity of the opening leader. In order to qualify for the Hall of Fame, therefore, an opening lead must be based on a logical and well-thought-out line of reasoning. The following hand is a good illustration of this principle; West was Irving Kass.

NORTH
♠ A 2
♡ 8 6
◊ A 9 5
♣ A K Q J 9 6

WEST
♠ J 7 6 3
♡ Q 10 9 2
◊ K 4
♣ 4 3 2

EAST
♠ Q 10 5 4
♡ A J 7 3
◊ 10 2
♣ 10 8 7

SOUTH
♠ K 9 8
♡ K 5 4
◊ Q J 8 7 6 3
♣ 5

The bidding:

NORTH	EAST	SOUTH	WEST
2 ♣	Pass	3 ◊	Pass
4 ♣	Pass	4 ◊	Pass
4 NT	Pass	5 ♣	Pass
6 ◊	Pass	Pass	Pass

Kass made the remarkable lead of the four of diamonds, and thereby gave declarer a serious problem. South couldn't believe that West would lead away from the trump king, and a losing finesse at trick one would allow the opponents to cash the heart ace and beat the slam very quickly. Therefore, South put up dummy's diamond ace and cashed the ace, king and queen of clubs, discarding two hearts when East followed suit. He now played dummy's club jack, planning to discard his last heart if East ruffed with the diamond king. If instead East held the two remaining trumps and chose to ruff with the ten, South would overruff, re-enter dummy with the spade ace, and lead another club, discarding his last heart while East ruffed with the high trump. East did in fact ruff with the ten of diamonds and South overruffed, but West overruffed with the king and led a heart to East's ace to beat the slam.

Declarer missed a point that was not lost upon Mr. Kass. South's 5 ♣ response to Blackwood showed no aces, so the trump ace had to be with North or East. In either case, the low diamond lead was most unlikely to cost a trick and could easily steer declarer away from the winning trump finesse—which is just what happened.

The following lead caused quite a sensation when it was made in the 1958 World Championships. Pietro Forquet, the Italian expert considered by many to be the world's greatest player, was in the West seat.

NORTH
♠ A K 8 4
♡ A 7 6 3 2
♢ 5
♣ A J 8

WEST
♠ 10 6 5 3 2
♡ 9
♢ A J 10 8 7 4 3
♣ —

EAST
♠ Q J 9
♡ 10 5
♢ K Q 2
♣ K Q 6 5 4

SOUTH
♠ 7
♡ K Q J 8 4
♢ 9 6
♣ 10 9 7 3 2

The bidding:

EAST	SOUTH	WEST	NORTH
1 NT	2 ♡	2 ♠	3 ♠
Pass	3 NT	5 ♢	5 ♡
Pass	Pass	Double	Pass
Pass	Pass		

In the system used by East-West, an opening 1 NT bid showed 12-17 points and a five-card club suit. Forquet was understandably eager to put his partner on lead quickly and obtain a club ruff before his sole trump was drawn, and he was pessimistic about his chances of success in the spade suit because of North's 3 ♠ cue-bid and East's failure to make a lead-directing double. Since one opponent was very likely to hold no more than a singleton diamond, Forquet led the diamond three! East won and returned a low club for West to ruff, and East later scored a club trick to beat the doubled contract.

Without the inspired lead of a low diamond, the hand is cold (and was duly made by the Italian declarer in the other room). Suppose West leads the ace of diamonds and shifts to a spade. Dummy wins and a low spade is ruffed, South cashes two high trumps and ruffs his last diamond in dummy, and cashes the spade king (pitching a club) and ruffs a spade. Declarer then leads a low club to dummy's eight, and East wins but is forced to make a most unhappy choice. He must either concede a ruff and discard or lead into North's club tenace, allowing declarer to bring home his contract.

Another lead from the 1958 World Championships was even more inspired but occasioned less acclaim, undoubtedly because it was vitiated by an uncooperative partner. West was the late Sidney Silodor, and let's look at the problem as he saw it.

WEST	NORTH	EAST	SOUTH
Pass	Pass	2 ♡	2 ♠
4 ♡	4 ♠	5 ♡	Pass
Pass	5 ♠	Pass	Pass
Pass			

Silodor held:

♠ J 8 6   ♡ A 9 6 2   ◇ Q 10 7 2   ♣ J 2

His partner's 2 ♡ opening was a weak two-bid, showing a good six-card suit and perhaps one high card on the side but not enough strength to open the bidding with 1 ♡. Prospects of defeating the contract appeared dismal, for only one round of hearts at most could survive the enemy's ruffing power, but Silodor was not one to give up easily. If East were to hold the diamond ace and South the king, declarer might misguess in diamonds and give the defenders two diamond tricks in addition to one heart trick, but it was necessary to act quickly before declarer obtained any discards. After all, if East did have the ace of diamonds in addition to his good heart suit, he could not hold any high cards in the black suits or he would be far too strong for his weak two-bid. Accordingly, Silodor made the brilliant opening lead of the nine of hearts. The complete deal:

NORTH
♠ K 9 3
♡ 8
◇ J 6 5 3
♣ A Q 10 9 5

WEST
♠ J 8 6
♡ A 9 6 2
◇ Q 10 7 2
♣ J 2

EAST
♠ 10
♡ K Q 10 7 5 3
◇ A 8 4
♣ 8 7 3

SOUTH
♠ A Q 7 5 4 2
♡ J 4
◇ K 9
♣ K 6 4

East won the opening heart lead, and had he shifted to a low diamond, declarer would probably have gone wrong and played small. South would reason that if East had the three top heart

honors, as would seem likely from the play to the first trick, he
could not hold the diamond ace or else he would have opened the
bidding with 1 ♡. Unfortunately, East laid down the diamond ace
at trick two, and declarer had no further problems.

The following stellar defense was the late Albert H. Morehead's. Although the critical plays involved the first two tricks,
only a born quibbler could take issue at the inclusion of this hand
in the Hall.

NORTH
♠ Q J 8 3
♡ J 7 5
◇ Q 7 2
♣ 9 7 4

WEST
♠ A K 7 2
♡ 10 8 4
◇ 10 9 5
♣ A Q 2

EAST
♠ 10 6 5 4
♡ 9 2
◇ K 4
♣ J 10 8 6 3

SOUTH
♠ 9
♡ A K Q 6 3
◇ A J 8 6 3
♣ K 5

The bidding:

SOUTH	WEST	NORTH	EAST
1 ♡	Pass	1 NT	Pass
2 ◇	Pass	2 ♡	Pass
4 ♡	Pass	Pass	Pass

South must lose two clubs and one spade as the cards lie,
but is likely to make his contract if left to his own devices. The
only chance to avoid a diamond loser is to lead a low diamond to
the jack and then cash the ace, hoping to bring down a doubleton
king in the East hand. As you can see, this play would be quite
successful.

Morehead, however, had paid careful attention to South's 2 ◊ bid and decided to give declarer a gentle push in the wrong direction. He opened the spade ace and shifted to the *nine* of diamonds. Declarer, who had been glumly pondering the chances of picking up the whole diamond suit without loss, perked up at this apparently favorable shift. He placed West with ◊ 9 5 and East with ◊ K 10 4, and therefore covered West's nine with dummy's queen and topped East's king with the ace. South now played the ace and king of hearts and led a low heart to dummy's jack, and returned a low diamond and finessed the eight. He was astonished when Morehead unexpectedly produced the diamond ten, and the two club tricks later collected by the defense produced a well-earned one-trick set.

Underleading an ace takes a strong heart, but underleading A K Q J takes nerves of steel. The heroine of the next deal was Mrs. A. H. Woods.

NORTH
♠ A 9 8 4
♡ A K J 4
◊ J 5
♣ 7 6 4

WEST
♠ J 7 3
♡ 3 2
◊ —
♣ A K Q J 8 5 3 2

EAST
♠ 10
♡ 10 9 8 5
◊ A K 10 7 6 4 2
♣ 10

SOUTH
♠ K Q 6 5 2
♡ Q 7 6
◊ Q 9 8 3
♣ 9

The bidding:

WEST	NORTH	EAST	SOUTH
1 ♣	Double	3 ◊	4 ♠
Pass	Pass	Pass	

Mrs. Woods correctly reasoned that it might well be essential to get East on lead quickly, and opened the deuce of clubs. A picture of East's expression when the club ten held the first trick would be a truly memorable keepsake, but he was not too taken aback to produce the winning defense. He cashed the two top diamonds, West discarding the three and deuce of hearts, and returned a heart for West to ruff and defeat the contract.

In Chapter 9, the judicious lead of an unsupported honor was cited as an example of expert technique. Here's an illustration from the 1967 World Championships with Alvin Roth in the spotlight.

NORTH
♠ K 10 6 3
♡ 9 2
◇ K 9 6
♣ A J 9 5

WEST
♠ Q 7 2
♡ K 10 8 7
◇ 5
♣ 10 8 7 6 4

EAST
♠ A J 9 5 4
♡ Q 6 4
◇ Q 10 8 3
♣ Q

SOUTH
♠ 8
♡ A J 5 3
◇ A J 7 4 2
♣ K 3 2

The bidding:

EAST	SOUTH	WEST	NORTH
Pass	1 ◇	Pass	1 ♠
Pass	2 ◇	Pass	3 ♣
Pass	3 NT	Pass	Pass
Pass			

With perfect defense, the lead of any spade will defeat the contract, but Roth's outstanding lead of the spade queen made

things easy for partner (and very tough for declarer). South
assumed that West also had the spade jack and ducked the first
trick in dummy, and Roth continued with a low spade to
dummy's ten and East's jack. East shifted to a heart, which South
ducked; West won with the ten and returned a spade, allowing
East to run the suit. The eventual result was down three; the hand
can actually be made by perfect play after the "normal" heart
lead. In the other room, the Americans played 3 NT from the
North seat after a light opening bid of 1 ♠ by East and made the
contract, giving the U.S. team a handsome gain on this hand.

   The play made by West in the next deal is not uncommon at
later stages of a hand when the defenders can see the dummy, but
is most unusual when accomplished on opening lead.

NORTH
♠ 10 9 7
♡ 10 9 5
◇ 9 7 2
♣ A J 9 5

WEST   EAST
♠ K   ♠ 5 4 3 2
♡ 8 6 4 3 2   ♡ 7
◇ Q 8 5   ◇ 6 4 3
♣ K 8 7 3   ♣ Q 10 6 4 2

SOUTH
♠ A Q J 8 6
♡ A K Q J
◇ A K J 10
♣ —

The bidding:

SOUTH	WEST	NORTH	EAST
2 ♠	Pass	2 NT	Pass
3 ♡	Pass	3 ♠	Pass
4 ◇	Pass	5 ♣	Pass
5 ◇	Pass	5 ♠	Pass
6 ♠	Pass	Pass	Pass

West kept a keen ear tuned to the bidding, and deduced that North had the club ace for his 5 ♣ bid. It was also clear that South, who had bid three suits, was very short in clubs and might easily be void. Ordinarily, this would make clubs a poor lead, for declarer would get a free finesse if dummy held the ace-queen, but West was desperately concerned about his singleton spade king. It was quite conceivable that South could never get to dummy, in which case he would have no choice but to lay down the ace of spades. This gruesome possibility was to be avoided at all costs, so West led a low club. Declarer gratefully put up dummy's ace and took the spade finesse, and West later scored the diamond queen to set the slam.

The name of the hero of the next deal is unfortunately lost to posterity, but his false-card is extremely impressive. It was amply rewarded, for it caused the defeat of a grand slam.

NORTH
♠ Q 9
♡ A 9 5 4
◇ K 10 8 7 6
♣ 10 4

WEST
♠ J 8 7 4 2
♡ J 3 2
◇ 9 3 2
♣ 9 2

EAST
♠ 10 5 3
♡ 10 7 6
◇ 5 4
♣ K 7 6 5 3

SOUTH
♠ A K 6
♡ K Q 8
◇ A Q J
♣ A Q J 8

The bidding:

SOUTH	WEST	NORTH	EAST
4 NT	Pass	7 NT	Pass
Pass	Pass		

This hand took place in a 1959 Pennsylvania tournament. South's 4 NT opening bid is hardly an everyday occurrence, but North was not confused. Puzzle: With twelve top tricks, the club king onside, and the hearts breaking 3-3, how did declarer go down in 7 NT? The solution is quite simple; West led the *jack* of hearts! South now decided that it was no longer necessary to risk the club finesse, and after playing off various winners eventually led the queen of hearts and followed with the heart eight, confidently finessing dummy's nine because West was "sure" to have the ten for his opening lead.

Down one.

Hindsight always provides clearer vision, but the lead of the jack of hearts—or any heart, for that matter—from J 10 3 2 against 7 NT would be shocking by a good player, which West apparently was. On the other hand, the lead from J 3 2, while most unusual, would be less likely to give up a trick. Had this occurred to declarer, he might have thought again about the "obvious" heart finesse—but then again, he would have spoiled an excellent story.

APPENDIX

Modern Lead Conventions

♠ ♡ ◇ ♣

Many experts have found through experience that the "standard" card choices for opening leads (as summarized in Chapter 2) often pose insuperable problems for the leader's partner. Therefore, they have devised various new techniques to overcome these difficulties. Some of the new procedures have unfortunately created as many problems as they have solved, but others are extremely effective. If you adopt the best of these methods for your own use, you will have an additional edge over players using standard leads. Also, other players are likely to use these conventions against you, and your declarer play will profit if you are familiar with the meaning of their leads. Be sure to note, however, that these conventions apply only to the opening lead at trick one, and standard methods are used at later stages of the hand; and the opponents are entitled to know about any conventional treatment that you use.

LOW LEAD FROM THREE SMALL

Procedure: Holding three small cards, lead the lowest. From 8 6 3, lead the three. (The "standard" lead would be the eight.)

Advantages: (1) Partner will find it easier to recognize the lead of a moderately high spot-card as a singleton or doubleton, since you will lead the eight from a singleton or from 8 6 but not from 8 6 3. (2) When you lead low from three small, declarer may be misled into thinking that you have some length and strength in the suit. The "top of nothing" lead, on the other hand, is more likely to pinpoint any missing honors in partner's hand.

Disadvantages: (1) Partner will find it harder to recognize the lead of a low spot-card as a singleton or doubleton. Suppose that the deuce is led, dummy has Q J 6, and partner holds A K 10 8 7 4. His king tops dummy's jack, and declarer follows with the three. Playing standard leads, partner has no problem; you would lead the top card from a doubleton or worthless tripleton, so the deuce must be a singleton. Playing low leads from three small, partner may go wrong, for you could have either a singleton or 9 5 2. (2) Partner, instead of declarer, may be misled into thinking that you have some length and strength in the suit. After a standard "top of nothing" lead, he is more likely to look elsewhere for your high cards. (3) When you lead "top of nothing," you can sometimes false-card to your advantage by playing the lowest card on the next round of the suit. This may convince declarer that you began with a doubleton and induce him to ruff with a high trump on the next round of the suit, which may establish a trick for the defense. If you lead low from three small, however, it is impossible to deceive declarer in this way.

Recommendation: This convention is neither much worse nor much better than the standard "top of nothing" procedure.

"MUD"

Procedure: Holding three small cards, lead the middle one and play the highest card on the next round of the suit. For example, lead the six from 8 6 3 and play the eight next time. The convention derives its name from the order of plays in the suit (**M**iddle, **U**p, **D**own). Note that with three to an honor, such as 10 7 3, the standard lead of the lowest card is correct.

Advantages: (1) The opening leader retains the option of either playing his highest card at the second trick to deny a doubleton, or false-carding with his lowest spot to deceive declarer. (2) If the opening lead can be recognized as the highest outstanding spot-card, then the leader's partner can be sure that the lead is *not* from three small. For example, if the seven is led, dummy has K J 8, and partner has A Q 9 5 4, he can be certain that you have at most a doubleton.

Disadvantages: (1) Making the same lead from Q 8 7, 8 7 3, or 7 3 puts quite a strain on partner, who may have great difficulty determining your holding in the suit. (2) If you decide to false-card by playing your lowest card at the second trick, you must do so quickly. If you hesitate, declarer will know that you have at least two remaining cards in the suit. (It is unethical to hesitate with a singleton to fool declarer; it is also unethical for partner to draw inferences from your hesitation.) It is often difficult to think fast enough to recognize a false-carding situation and act on it without giving the show away by a pause or fumble.

Recommendation: If you knew that the most important consideration on a given hand was to advise partner of your honor-card holding in the suit led, you would lead top of nothing and low from three to an honor. If a little bird advised you that partner needed to know whether you were very short in the suit or had three or more cards in it, you would lead low from three small. "MUD" is, in effect, a compromise between these two approaches. Like any compromise, it is not as good as either of the other methods at their best, nor as bad as either of the other methods at their worst. "MUD" is best reserved for situations where keeping declarer in doubt is more important than giving information to partner.

ACE LEAD FROM ACE-KING

Procedure: Against suit contracts, with three or more cards in a suit including the ace and king, lead the ace. (This includes A K Q.) With ace-king doubleton, lead the king. This is exactly the opposite of the standard procedure. Holding king-queen (but not the ace), lead the king as in standard methods.

Advantages: Using standard leads, the king is led from both ace-king and king-queen. This can create some awesome problems for the leader's partner, as in the following examples:

(a)	DUMMY		(b)	DUMMY	
	♠ 8 5 2			♠ 8 5 2	
		YOU			YOU
♠ K led		♠ J 7 4	♠ K led		♠ 7 4

In hand (a), you certainly don't want partner to continue the suit if he has led from ace-king and give declarer an undeserved trick with ♠ Q 6 3. You should therefore signal with the four, discouraging partner from continuing the suit and planning to gain the lead later and lead through declarer's queen. (If partner has led from A K Q, he will continue spades regardless of your signal, since he needs no help from you.) However, if partner has led from the king-queen, you want partner to continue the suit if declarer ducks the first trick, for a shift may give declarer time to set up a side suit for some spade discards. In this case, your proper signal is the seven-spot. Without a handy crystal ball or ouija board, you cannot possibly tell what to do. Similarly, in case (b), you can get a third-round ruff if partner has led from the ace-king and so should signal with your seven. If partner has led from king-queen, however, a wily declarer may duck with A J 6 and obtain an extra spade trick when partner duly continues the suit in response to your signal.

These are just two of the horrendous situations that arise from leading the king from both ace-king and king-queen. The ace from ace-king convention resolves these problems neatly. In hand (a), you can confidently signal with the seven if partner leads the king, for his lead shows the queen; and you should discourage with the four if partner leads the ace, showing ace-king. In hand (b), play the four if partner leads the king, and encourage with the seven if he leads the ace. Note that when this convention is played and the king is led, the leader's partner should usually *not* signal high with a small doubleton. Encouragement should be given only with the ace or jack.

Disadvantages: The lead of the ace from ace-king substitutes one problem for another. The leader's partner can differentiate ace-king from king-queen, but cannot distinguish between an unsupported ace and ace-king. When an ace is led, therefore, the leader's partner may have trouble planning the defensive strategy.

Recommendation: Players who use this convention tend to shy away from the lead of an unsupported ace even when it is correct, for fear that partner will read them for ace-king. Since there is a third method that is superior to both standard methods and the ace from ace-king convention, there is no reason to pay the price of potential confusion when an ace is led.

RUSINOW LEADS

Procedure: Against suit contracts, with three or more cards in a suit, lead the *lower* of two touching honors. With any doubleton, lead the top card. For example:

Holding:	Lead:
A K 7 6 5; A K Q 3	King
K Q 8; K Q J 10	Queen
Q J 9 8	Jack
J 10 9 5	Ten
10 9 3	Nine
9 8 2; 9 7 4	Second highest
A K; K Q; Q J; Q 5; J 10; J 3; 10 9; 10 2; 9 4	Top card

Rusinow leads should *not* be used in a suit bid by partner. After a king lead, the leader's partner should signal encouragement by playing a high spot if he holds the queen or a doubleton and wishes the suit continued.* After a queen lead, the leader's partner should signal encouragement if he holds the ace or jack, but should *discourage* partner from continuing the suit if he holds a doubleton by playing the *smaller* card so as to keep partner from losing a trick if declarer, holding ace-jack-small, ducks the first round. (Rusinow leads are named after their inventor, Sydney Rusinow.)

Advantages: (1) Rusinow leads eliminate the ambiguities found in both standard leads and the lead of the ace from ace-king. The ace shows the ace alone; the king is led from ace-king; and the queen from king-queen. (2) A doubleton honor can be

---

* Exception: The play of the queen under the king guarantees possession of the jack and asks partner to underlead his ace on the next trick. Therefore, you should *never* play the queen from queen-small.

clearly defined. If West leads the king and follows with the queen, dummy has 8 5 2, and East has A 7 6 3, West must have a doubleton if he is using the Rusinow approach because he has led the king without the ace. East can therefore overtake the queen and give him a ruff. Using standard leads, East could not afford to overtake for fear of establishing declarer's jack if West began with K Q 4.

Disadvantages: Ambiguity may arise in some situations. For example, the lead of jack may be from jack doubleton (or jack singleton) rather than queen-jack.

Recommendation: Rusinow leads are unquestionably superior to both standard leads and the lead of the ace from ace-king, and are recommended for your adoption.

JOURNALIST LEADS

Procedure: (1) *Against suit contracts:* (i) Rusinow honor-card leads are used. That is, lead the lower of two touching honors in a suit not bid by partner. (ii) The lowest card is led from an odd number, and the third-best card is led from an even number, when leading a low card. For example:

Holding:	*Lead:*
K 8 6	Six
K 8 6 3	Six
K 8 6 3 2	Two
K 8 6 4 3 2	Six
K 8 6 5 4 3 2	Two

(2) *Against notrump contracts:* (i) The lead of the jack denies a higher honor in the suit, whereas the lead of the ten indicates an interior sequence and shows an honor higher than the jack. The nine is led from 10 9 8. Thus, lead the jack from J 10 9 8 3, but lead the ten from A J 10 9 3, K J 10 9 4, A 10 9 8 3, K 10 9 7 3, or Q 10 9 8 5. (ii) As was discussed in Chapter 2, the lead of an ace asks partner to unblock an honor if he has one or signal his length if he does not (high card from even, low from odd) so that

the leader can tell whether or not the suit will run. (iii) The fourth-best rule is abandoned. Instead, if your whole hand suggests that partner *should* return your suit when he gains the lead, lead a low spot-card (such as the deuce, three, or four). If instead your hand suggests that partner should not return your suit unless his holding in it is very strong, lead a high spot-card (such as the eight or seven).

These leads derive their name from the fact that they were developed by the staff of *The Bridge Journal,* a magazine for advanced players published between 1963 and 1966.

Advantages: (1) The advantages of Rusinow honor-card leads against suit contracts have already been discussed. (2) The lead of the third-best card from an even number and lowest card from an odd number against suit contracts is extremely useful to the leader's partner, who often desperately needs a count in the suit. For example, suppose that declarer is playing 6 ♠ and the club suit is distributed as follows:

                      Dummy
                      ♣ Q J 6
          ♣ 3 led   You
                      ♣ A K 9 4

You top dummy's jack with your king, and declarer plays the five. You would greatly enjoy beating the slam by cashing your ace, but if declarer's five-spot is singleton he will ruff the ace and may obtain a crucial discard on dummy's queen. On the other hand, if you shift and declarer did have another club, he may be able to discard it on a side suit and make his slam. What to do? Standard leads offer no help, for partner could have 10 8 7 3 or 10 8 7 3 2. Playing Journalist leads, however, you are certain that you can cash a second round of clubs, for partner would lead the deuce from 10 8 7 3 2. There are many situations like this, especially in tournament play where cashing every trick is critical. (3) The lead of the jack to deny a higher honor and the ten to show an honor higher than the jack, against notrump contracts, resolves an extremely troublesome ambiguity in standard methods. Here's a hand which illustrates the advantage of this Journalist Lead technique:

NORTH (dummy)
♠ A J 10 3 2
♡ 6
◇ 7 3
♣ A K 10 7 4

◇ 10 led   EAST (you)
                            ♠ Q 9 6 5
                            ♡ Q J 10 9
                            ◇ A 4 2
                            ♣ Q 2

The bidding:

NORTH	EAST	SOUTH	WEST
1 ♣	Pass	1 ♡	Pass
1 ♠	Pass	3 NT	Pass
Pass	Pass		

Using standard leads, East is in a terrible predicament. If the diamond ten is from an interior sequence and South holds a hand such as

♠ K 4   ♡ A K 7 5 3   ◇ Q J 5   ♣ 6 5 3

then East can beat the contract simply by winning his ace and returning his partner's suit.* If, however, the ten is the top of a sequence and declarer holds

♠ K 4   ♡ K 7 5 3   ◇ K Q J   ♣ J 6 5 3

then this defense hands declarer his contract. South will win the diamond and play the ace and king of clubs, since he cannot afford to risk losing a club finesse to East and getting a heart return through his king, and easily make his contract. To beat the hand, East must win the first trick and shift to the heart queen.

---

* West must duck the second round of diamonds, however. If he carelessly wins the king and plays a third round, South will win and lead a low club to the ten, establishing the suit without permitting West to gain the lead, and East will not have a diamond to play.

Things are much better if the defenders are using Journalist Leads. If West leads the ten, East knows that he has an interior sequence and plays ace and another diamond. From 10 9 8 6, West leads the nine, which promises the ten but no honor higher than the ten. East knows that he must look elsewhere for tricks, and puts up the ace and shifts to the queen of hearts. (4) Against notrump contracts, it is usually more important to advise partner whether or not to return your suit than it is to announce the exact number of cards that you hold. Using standard methods, partner may have a very tough time trying to determine if you have led the seven from Q 10 8 7 3 or 7 4 3, and a large number of points may ride on his decision. Using Journalist leads, you would lead the three from the first holding to encourage the return of the suit, and select the seven with the second holding to discourage the return of the suit. Similarly, if you must lead from a holding such as 10 6 2, lead the six. This is just good bridge, not a convention; the ten is too valuable a card to waste and the deuce would look too much like a lead from length. Playing Journalist leads, however, increases the odds that your lead will be read correctly, for it is unlikely that partner will interpret the six as a low spot whether or not it could conceivably be fourth-best.

Disadvantages: Journalist leads are not superior to standard leads in all situations; no convention works one hundred per cent of the time. Declarer may profit from the information provided by the lead, and in certain infrequent situations partner may be in doubt as to the leader's holding. The disadvantages, however, are remarkably few.

Recommendation: Journalist leads are a great improvement over standard leads and represent the best methods currently available. They are strongly recommended for your use, and will be well worth the time needed to commit them to memory.

OTHER CONVENTIONS

The Fisher Double: This is a special lead-directing double devised by Dr. John W. Fisher, and applies when the opponents open the bidding with 1 NT and subsequently play in 3 NT. If they have *not* used a Stayman 2 ♣ response, a double of the final contract requests a club lead. If they *have* used Stayman, a double of the final contract requests a diamond lead. The main advantage of this convention is that the opening leader knows exactly what is expected of him, and there is no possibility of ambiguity. After the auction 1 NT–3 NT, the Lightner double can be used regardless of what suit you want led, and is therefore preferable with a capable partner who will judge correctly most of the time. After other auctions, however, it is reasonable to employ the Fisher double.

Queen from A K Q: Some players lead the queen against suit contracts from A K Q. This enables partner to signal with the jack from jack-ten, allowing the opening leader to underlead his honors if he wishes his partner to be on lead. This is not an unreasonable convention, but is hardly essential. Playing the recommended Journalist or Rusinow leads, you can always choose to lead the queen from A K Q if you wish partner to signal with the jack; all you lose is that partner will not signal high with a doubleton.

Index